THE
Super Highway
IN UPSTATE
South Carolina

SCOTT WITHROW & WILLIAM DUNCAN

THE
History
PRESS

Published by The History Press
Charleston, SC
www.historypress.com

Copyright © 2025 by Scott Withrow and William Duncan
All rights reserved

First published 2025

Manufactured in the United States

ISBN 9781467158237

Library of Congress Control Number: 2024949882

I dedicate this book to my wife, Ann Dillard Withrow, and her knowledge of local history, especially peach-growing history. I dedicate it also to my late relatives: parents Sherwood and Mae Hamrick Withrow, Aunt Cleo Withrow Elam and first cousin Janet Withrow Walker. All enjoyed traveling as I do and would have enjoyed the book. Aunt Cleo, as a young woman from the Appalachian foothills, worked her way through Asheville Normal and Collegiate Institute and Columbia University. She subsequently traveled in her early '50s Dodge Gyromatic to work as a dietitian or teach home economics in such diverse places as Kansas State University (Manhattan), Berea College and the University of Delaware. I thought about Aunt Cleo when I hiked in Konza Prairie near Manhattan, Kansas.

I dedicate the book, also, to those historians and writers before me: to the late Anne McCuen, Mann Batson and Dean Campbell. I am inspired along the way by the writing of Anne Peden (*Highway 25 in the Carolinas*), Drew Hines (*Hidden History of the Dark Corner*) and Joada P. Hiatt and Ray Belcher (books on Greer).

—Scott Withrow

I wish to dedicate this book to my late grandparents, William Perry Duncan, Hattie Langford Duncan and Hettie Messick Daniel. They laid the foundation for my love of history by telling me stories from family history. My grandmother left me all of her research on our family history. I also dedicate this book to my late parents, William Ford Duncan and Etta Mae Daniel Duncan. They took me to countless historic sites while I was growing up. I must also dedicate this book to the late Mr. Bill Mosely and Mrs. Delia Moseley, who were my high school history teachers at Travelers Rest High School (SC), and Dr. A.V. Huff Jr. (former professor of history, vice president and dean at Furman University). Because of the inspiration provided by all of these people in my life, I am still studying history today.

—William (Lynn) Duncan

CONTENTS

ACKNOWLEDGEMENTS

W e want to begin by thanking Paul Green, who met with us at least five times. I learned much about Greer, especially its businesses, over a number of breakfasts at a favorite restaurant. Paul has a memory for history. Steven C. Hawkins, president of Western Carolina Railway, was as helpful as anyone, always making time and giving access to his collection of P&N Railway history.

We called on the following persons more than once for information. They were always helpful and helped make my thinking clearer and more focused: Shirley Beacham, Wes Breedlove, Lemuel Dillard, Tony Dillard, Dr. Drew Hines, Dr. A.V. Huff, Tommy Hughes, Sonny Rhem, Richard Sawyer and Dr. Donna Haisty Winchell. Franky Dillard spoke of his grandparents, who lived along the National Highway in Taylors. Richard Vaughn spoke of agriculture and sometimes isolation from events such as construction of the Super Highway.

Doug Edwards recalled by phone early farm life just off the Super Highway near the Hampton Massacre marker. Rose Marie Jordan also contributed to landownership in that area. Rose Marie is a treasure when it comes to Greer history. Gail Hemphill Snow spoke of her youth and playing in a field with other children with a view of the Super Highway, that field now changed to housing.

Also, we met or communicated with some people we might not have otherwise had contact with except for interviews for this book. These include Fred Bagwell on Chick Springs history, Mike Boone on the Super Highway in the Bob Jones University area, Tiger O'Rourke on the area near Henry's Smokehouse, Ernest Everett Blevins on the National Highway, Donna Chandler on family memories of what became the El Matador Restaurant, cousins Mike Reynolds and Jeff Mace (and also Janet Fleming-Smith) on Southern Worsted, Dot Arms on Lyman about such topics as Lyman Printing and Finishing and traveling to Greer on the P&N Railway and Jennifer Tucker Griffith with permission to use a photo of her late uncle in the median of the Super Highway. I connected with Chick Springs historian Bill Wilson through longtime acquaintance Anita Painter. Lee Mitchell, hydrogeologist, shed much light on springs and spring history. Steve Frady is one of the few people who remembers construction of the Super Highway. He was only four or five when they finished the Lyman section in 1946, but he remembered the big machinery. Richard Lane remembered much about Greer businesses, especially the Fork Restaurant. Tony Waters added much since his parents owned and ran the Fork Restaurant. Skip Davenport of D&D Motors provided Greer history and contacts. The owners of Red Hill Hot Dogs and Hilda Howard Morrow of Days of Pacific Mills: A Lyman Group (Facebook) contributed to my understanding of the Lyman-Wellford-Duncan area. Others contributed to property and genealogical understanding. These include Joel Waddell and Joye Waddell Leopard on the Waddell-Raines-Tolbert-McCarter families in the area of White Oak Baptist Church, Bob Jones University and Woodlawn Memorial Park. Larry Conant helped find land records associated with the present Greer City Park on land once situated along the "Indian Boundary Line."

Two authors replied to my queries (authors don't have to do that) or otherwise communicated with me: Martin T. Olliff, author of *Getting Out of the Mud: The Alabama Good Roads Movement and Highway Administration, 1898–1928*, and Richard F. Weingroff, the Federal Highway Administration's "unofficial historian." Thanks to each for their interest in the Super Highway project. Dan Smith, author of *Texas Number I: The Bankhead Highway in Texas*, gave me much good information on the entire National Highway. His book serves as a guide for my writing on the National Highway. Terry Shelswell of the Military Vehicle Preservation Association filled in information about the 2015 reenactment of the 1920 National Highway convoy.

Dr. Thomas McAbee proofread and offered needed changes to the chapter on the National Highway. Thanks to Ray Belcher for putting me in contact with Dr. McAbee. I have always respected Joada Hiatt for her knowledge of history and writing, and I called on her to proofread the chapter on Super Highway businesses. Dr. Donna Haisty Winchell somehow worked it in with her own textbook revision to proofread a number of chapters, especially the one on Chick Springs. Dr. Larry Greer spent precious time proofreading the chapter "Native Americans." Working with Larry always reminded me of his father, the late Bill Greer, who volunteered at the Roper Mountain Science Center Living History Farm when I was curator/manager. Steven D. Smith, research professor, South Carolina Institute for Archaeology and Anthropology, also offered pertinent suggestions, especially related to the terminology. Karolyn Taylor proofread the chapter on Chick Springs. Karolyn, who remembered swimming at the Chick Springs pool, was a wealth of information. I discovered that her great-grandfather was Alfred Taylor, the namesake of Taylors, South Carolina, and that Karolyn's father heard many stories of the Civil War, Chick Springs and other topics in the Alfred Taylor home. It stood where Taylors First Baptist Church is now located, the land for the church donated by the Taylor family.

Others provided tours or access to libraries or museums. Nathan Majewski of White Oak Baptist Church took down upper-shelf displayed collection plates made of white oak so I could photograph them. Nathan was a fountain of information on the Super Highway in the church's area, and he couldn't have been more gracious in showing me photos and other items in the church museum. Donald Jones of the Tucapau-Startex Foundation took time out from his busy schedule to give me a tour of the Wellford-Clevedale section of the Super Highway, portions of the earlier National Highway (Old Spartanburg Highway) and the Tucapau-Startex textile community. He and others are doing splendid work at Tucapau-Startex. John Montogomery, Benson Alfa Romeo and Fiat studio manager, deserves praise for his excellent tour of Benson Memory Lane Museum

Bob Dicey provided information on World War I Camps Sevier (Greenville) and Wadsworth (Spartanburg), as well as proofreading our article on the camps. Raymond Brown shared information about the Southern Railway. Joseph Hudson volunteered to scan railway-related materials and photographs. Harry Corrigan shared information about his father, Douglas "Wrong Way" Corrigan's 1938 flight from New York to Ireland. Information about the peach industry in Spartanburg was provided by Mac McMillin and Craig Myers.

The following provided photos and other images and permissions for use: Joanna Beasley (archivist and technical services librarian, North Greenville University), Mike Boone, Olivia Brittain-Toole (reference specialist, Special Collections and Archives, Clemson University), Greg Burns, Peter Butchart (Rudolf Anderson Jr. American Legion Post 214 Cecil D. Buchanan Museum of Military History), *Cardboard America* (Colonial Court Motel), Donna Chandler, Bob Dicey (The Military History Center of Carolinas), Janet Fleming-Smith, Paul Green, Carole Greene Henderson (Carole's Record Shop), Alan Hiatt, Rick Jones (manager, Digital Collections Center, James B. Duke Library, Furman University), Don Koonce, David Lovegrove (Greer Heritage Museum), Jonathan Lovegrove (Greer Heritage Museum), Nathan Majewski, John Matzko (archivist, Bob Jones University), James B. McClary (South Carolina Law Enforcement Officers Hall of Fame), Sarah McFeely (map illustration), Hilda Howard Morrow, Mark Olencki (photographer/ digital images manager, Wofford College), Richard Sawyer (map and postcard), South Carolina Archives and History, Steven Varner (National Highway map) and Jake Whitmire (transportation planner, Appalachian Council of Governments).

Archivists at the SC Department of Archives and History and South Carolina Room (Greenville Library System) deserve special thanks. Personnel at the South Carolina Room, Greenville County Library, went out of their way to be helpful. Brad Steinecke, director of local history, Kennedy Room, Headquarters, Spartanburg County Library, provided images and information.

The project could not have been completed without the support of the Greer Heritage Museum and its director, David Lovegrove, and family members Jonathan Lovegrove and Bethany Lovegrove. Much thanks also to Chad Rhoad, senior acquisitions editor of The History Press, who was very patient in explaining the many moving parts in writing for publication.

Finally, and most importantly, I want to thank my wife, Ann Dillard Withrow, for her contributions on Greer history, especially peach history and her memories of businesses along the Super Highway. I thank her for her patience with my over-the-top enthusiasm (at times) for Super Highway history.

—Scott Withrow

INTRODUCTION

The Super Highway must have been big news regionwide. My family drove from North Carolina to try out the new highway from Spartanburg to Greenville. It was the mid-1950s, and I remember it to this day. Certain landmarks stand out: Culler-Jackson Furniture Store—we marveled at its size and inventory of furniture for sale. Maybe my family had heard of it; its owners advertised regionwide. I remember a hamburger and ice cream somewhere, perhaps a forerunner of Tab's Dairy Bar in Greer. We hunted a relative in Taylors, but we never found them. We did not have a current address, but I remember asking at more than one local business if they knew so-and-so. That is how it was done in those days—no Googling addresses or phone numbers, no GPS. It was that trip or a later one to Sears-Roebuck in Greenville where I marveled at—and rode—the escalator, likely the first I had seen.

I learned more about Greenville and the Super Highway when WFBC-TV (the call letters for First Baptist Church, where the station began in the basement) signed on the air on December 31, 1953, transmitting from a tower on Paris Mountain. For the first time, we could get more than WBTV in Charlotte. Via television, I grew up with Greenville and Monty's Rascals, Stowe Hoyle, Greenville's Soap Box Derby and the Super Highway, known variously as the Dual Lane Highway, Highway 29 and, for one portion, Wade Hampton Boulevard. It must have been in the early 1960s when I traveled the Super Highway with a group of friends from North Carolina to attend a race at the Greenville-Pickens Speedway, now a historic landmark itself. I pulled, of course, for Chevrolet driver Rex White, since my father drove a Chevrolet and I was beginning to drive. Later hiking trips in the mountains of South Carolina put me again on the Super Highway, where I remember quite a few traffic lights between Greenville and Greer to and from North Carolina.

Since my hometown in North Carolina was a little over thirty miles north of Spartanburg, I remember that city just as well and listening to Farmer Cliff Gray and his morning radio farm report and other WSPA-Radio personalities such as Jane Dalton, Elmo Fagg and the Blue Ridge Quartet and, later, Bill Drake and television personality Nancy Welch. I remember, too, the Steeple Restaurant, west of downtown Spartanburg along the Super Highway, and its onetime repurposing as a used car dealership. I remember peach orchards not far from the Super Highway in the Blackstock Road area where businesses now stand.

Moving to Greenville County in the late 1980s brought me in contact again with the Super Highway. It was a gradual process, but I learned more of its corridor history over the years—the remarkable history of Chick Springs, the National Highway, the building of the Super Highway and its businesses. I had the pleasure of briefly talking with local historians, now passed, especially Jean Martin Flynn and G.E. Corley Hendricks. I was a member of a history group with the late Anne K. McCuen, Dean Campbell and Mann Batson and talked with them often. My big regret is that I did not get interested earlier and talk with more people who remembered the Super Highway being built, knowledgeable people like the late E.D. Sloan and others. Likewise, I missed taking photos of buildings long ago torn down. But as I drive the road today, I wonder where earlier businesses were located, how the building of the road changed the landscape and if there is someone somewhere in their late eighties or nineties who remembers the building of a regionally known highway and its link to other places—the lore of its early days and people and businesses long gone.

I became interested, too, in the Super Highway's corridor history. My interest in Native American history is long-standing, but I also researched Chick Springs and its long history in the Taylors community. As much as anything, I enjoyed researching the 1916 and beyond National (Bankhead) Highway. My fascination with that route continues. In fact, we see similar themes expressed for road improvement coming with superhighways—the Super Highway in this instance—and later interstates. Textiles, so often associated with railways and communities along the National Highway and later Super Highway, cannot be left out.

I am sure my fascination with the Super Highway and its history goes back to my childhood, when I played with toy trucks and "road scrapers" and built roads of my own in the dirt. My view has matured, and I look at roads from a historical and environmental perspective. It is fascinating to study the progression from Native trails to wagon roads, to curvy rural roads and, later, to modern highways that often bisect the older roads. Today, I look at what highways have done to the environment and how they take up farmland and sometimes divide communities—in short, how they change a city or community. I notice more and more the ridges that the Super Highway bisects—looking like giant folds on the land—and the uphill-downhill nature of the highway from Spartanburg to Greenville. I think of the Super Highway, too, in terms of safety, and I realize that people have grieved over loss of life of friends and relatives on the highway. Like others I am sure, I have a love-hate relationship with overcrowded Highway 29, the Super Highway, the hate relationship more prevalent during rush hour. I travel it almost every day, and I do not pretend to have the answers to is improvement.

—Scott Withrow

PART I

BEFORE THE
SUPER HIGHWAY

Chapter 1

NATIVE AMERICANS

The area surrounding the Super Highway was hunting ground for prehistoric Native Woodland and Mississippian cultures. In the historic era, it was the land of Cherokee (and possibly Catawba) hunters and warriors. According to tradition, there was a terrible all-day battle between the Catawba and Cherokee. One version has it that when peace terms were agreed on, the Catawba were to occupy the land east of the Catawba River as hunting grounds and the Cherokee to the west. One version fixes the Broad River as the line between Cherokee and Catawba hunting grounds. There is some credence to that version, since the Catawba name for the Broad is *Eswa Huppeday*, or "line river."[1] Although there were likely Catawba incursions onto Cherokee hunting grounds, it is accurate to say that the hunting grounds now in Greenville and Spartanburg Counties were dominated by the Cherokee. But it would be a mistake to look for permanent Cherokee villages in the Greenville-Spartanburg area, especially along the Super Highway corridor. Those were found in the large river bottoms of present Oconee and Pickens County, much more conducive to growing corn, beans and squash—the three sisters in Native America.

The Cherokee Path, the main trading path with Charles Town (Charleston), led through what is today Anderson, Pickens and Oconee Counties. It was the main route for the deerskin trade wherein European settlers traded manufactured goods such as firearms, cloth, axes, hoes and brass kettles for deerskins obtained by Native Americans.[2] Fairly reliable statistics of the deerskin trade can be reconstructed from 1699 to 1765. They show that

Charles Town shipped an incredible number of deerskins to England. From 1699 to 1715, Charles Town shipped nearly 54,000 deerskins annually. Trade fluctuated due to Cherokee success in hunting, warfare and other factors, but the two decades after 1730 were excellent ones for Charles Town merchants. For example, in 1748, Charles Town shipped approximately 160,000 deerskins. By mid-century, the export value of deerskins roughly equaled the total of such products as indigo, lumber, naval stores and beef and pork.[3] The deerskin trade, however, encompassed the entire South Carolina upcountry. The area of the Super Highway corridor contained trails and hunting camps, the latter revisited often during Cherokee hunting trips eastward.[4]

Specific archaeological research is often missing for Greenville and Spartanburg Counties, and this is especially true of the Super Highway corridor. Much more site work has been done of prehistoric lifeways along the Savannah River basin as a context for study of the upstate.[5]

The Topper archaeological site in Allendale County has produced artifacts that some archaeologists believe indicate human habitation in the Americas earlier than the Clovis culture, perhaps as early as fifty thousand years ago.[6]

Important to Native-colonial relations was the need for a well-defined boundary line between the Cherokee and white settlements after the Cherokee War of 1759–61. The Crown appointed John Stuart as the Indian superintendent for the "Southern Department." Stuart called for a conference to settle the problems between the colonists and Native Americans.

In November 1763, four southern colonial governors and representatives of the Cherokee, Catawba, Chickasaw, Creek and Choctaw tribes met and signed the Treaty of Augusta. With this treaty, the tribes agreed to end their fighting. It was agreed also that the Catawba would be given a small fifteen-square-mile reservation near present-day Rock Hill, South Carolina. In addition, the treaty specified that a boundary line between the Cherokee lands and the colonists be surveyed. In 1766, the southern part of the border was surveyed from a point on the Reedy River to the Georgia border, now the present line between Abbeville and Anderson Counties.[7]

But the boundary from a point on the Reedy River north remained ill defined. A reliable demarcation came in 1767, when Governor Tryon of North Carolina had the line surveyed. His commissioners and surveyors started from some unknown point on the Reedy River (some think north of Fork Shoals and near the Great Cane Brake) and ran the boundary fifty-three miles north to Tryon Mountain near today's Tryon, North Carolina. A party of Cherokee under Ustenaka and Tryon's surveyors blazed certain

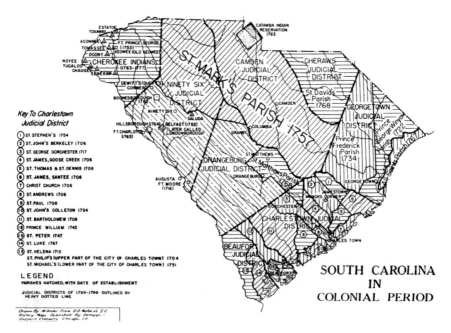

Map of the colonial period in South Carolina. *Courtesy of David Duncan Wallace Heirs.*

"boundary" trees, with the Cherokee blazing a symbol for Ustenaka's string of beads and Tryon's surveyors using the initials of the survey commissioners. Historian Louis De Vorsey Jr. wrote in 1966 that the "ravages of weather, disease, and the woodsman's blade" had removed all these trees and their carvings of over two centuries ago. Some of the boundary trees must have remained until at least the Civil War and even after, and for a time, local people could identify them.

The land east of the line, encompassing what was thought to be part of North Carolina at the time of the survey, was placed appropriately by De Vorsey in a chapter on the North Carolina–Cherokee boundary.[8] There are no known maps of the survey, but early deeds record "Ancient Boundary" or some similar term for those deeds adjoining the line.[9] Deeds backed up to the line from the east before Greenville was opened to white settlement, and afterward, others backed to the line from the west.

There were exceptions to settling beyond the boundary line. A South Carolina statute of 1739 made it illegal for a British citizen to own Indian land in the colony. Richard Pearis, a trader with the Cherokee, became the most notable exception to this rule. Pearis used underhanded tactics to get around this. He had progeny by his Virginia wife, Rhoda, and a son,

George, by a Cherokee woman. Working with his Cherokee son, he was able to obtain by questionable means twelve square miles of Cherokee land. Later, after 1770, Pearis settled on his Greenville land and established a plantation and a store at the Reedy River falls. To facilitate his trade with the Cherokee, he built Pearis Wagon Road, which ran west to the Saluda River.[10] As a British Loyalist during the American Revolution, he eventually had to flee his home for British-controlled East Florida and then to the Bahamas, where he lived out his life with other Loyalists.[11] His name remains as the variant spelling, Paris, in place names such as Paris School, the community of Paris, Paris Township and Paris Mountain. His redress for property with the British government is one of the first descriptions of the land that was to become Greenville. His landholdings reached west to the Saluda River and beyond. The wagon roads he built for Cherokee trade ran away from the boundary line.[12]

The twentieth-century east–west Super Highway bisected the former Indian Boundary Line, the straight-as-an-arrow line today dividing Spartanburg and Greenville Counties. Place names adjacent to the line in the Greer area reflect the Tryon Survey, including the former Tryon School, Tryon Street and Line Street. Frohock Creek, a tributary of the South Tyger River, has its headwaters near the Super Highway. Sounding to some like a tool or weapon—a combination of tomahawk and (shingle or riving) froe—it was named for John Frohock, one of the commissioners and surveyors of the Indian Boundary Line.[13] The fact that it is often spelled today as "Frohawk" is more in keeping with its perceived origin as a tool or weapon and obscures its real origin.

White families settling near or over the line faced Cherokee raids and captivity during times of conflict. Not all settlers were known, but some are recorded and stand out. The Hampton Massacre (Hampton Raid) of July 1776 serves up family legends and traditions associated with this story.[14] The capture of the eight-year-old family member John Bynum, later ransomed by his uncle Wade Hampton I (early 1750s–February 4, 1835) in 1777 after a settlement with the Cherokee, is a key part of the story. Bynum later became the surveyor general of South Carolina. Wade Hampton I was the grandfather of Wade Hampton III (1882–1902), Confederate general, South Carolina governor and U.S. senator and namesake of a portion of the Super Highway.

Such frontier conflict led to the Rutherford-Williamson punitive expedition against the Cherokee in 1776, in which four Hampton male relatives participated. As a result of the Treaty of Dewitt's Corner after

Frohock/Frohawk Creek near Greer. *Photo by Scott Withrow.*

the war, the Cherokee ceded to South Carolina what became Greenville, Oconee and Pickens Counties.[15] The Cherokee were forced into the far western part of the state, but some were still east of the mountains. It was a story not only of the Hamptons but also of Native resistance to white incursions on or near their tribal lands.[16] The Hampton monument stands today along the Super Highway near the site of the original Hampton farm near the South Tyger River.[17]

About five miles northwest of present downtown Greer, Indian trader Jacob Hite and family members were killed and others taken captive in a Cherokee raid in July 1776.[18] A few miles north of Highway 29 near the county line (Indian Boundary Line) is the plaque-set-in-stone marker for Woods Fort with the inscription, "1775, Near this site stood Woods Fort (1755?–1776?), a refuge for women and children from the Cherokee Indians."[19] There is much speculation, much of it informed, on the exact location of Woods Fort.

But there is a local history beyond the conflict and its modern-day markers. The Greer Heritage Museum has on display a collection of points (arrowheads or spear points) and tools found in the area. Although such collections are often associated with the Cherokee, many are classified as Mississippian, going back to the prehistoric chiefdoms prior to the historic-period Cherokee. Ray Belcher and Joada P. Hiatt, in *Greer: From Cotton Town to Industrial Center*, write that Greenville County educator and syndicated genealogist Leonardo Andrea found artifacts in William W. Burgess's hilltop peach orchard. Today, this hilltop or ridge is the site of the Burgess Hills development (aka Mount Vernon Estates) and offers a great view of the Super Highway facing east. The authors write about area stone knapping sites and cite Henry Clark's discovery of mostly Archaic-era stone axes, hoes and projectile points along Frohock/Frohawk Creek.[20]

Some of today's roads are a visible reminder of Native Americans, since many of the Native trails became the earliest roads. A good example is the Tugaloo Road north of Greer, part of the Great Indian Warpath running from the Tugaloo River to Virginia. Both McKelvey Road and Rutherford Road were closer to the Super Highway.[21] Native Americans undoubtably traveled via a well-worn trail to what became Chick Springs because of the spring's supposed medicinal properties.

Two local Greenville historians addressed the trails and their importance: Greenville resident Anne K. McCuen, an expert on deed research, discussed such trails as the Upper, Middle and Lower Indian Paths; the Toogoloo (Tugalo); and others in her book *Including a Pile of Rocks*. Lesser trails, one of them following a ridge between the South Tyger River and the Middle Tyger River and crossing the Greenville-Spartanburg line, led off one of the major trails. Importantly, McCuen noted that it was easiest for settlers, drovers and others to use the existing trails and make them into early roads. The State Road, begun in 1818 and completed in 1820, connected Lowcountry South Carolina with Appalachia, providing access to livestock drovers. Incorporating old Native trails at points, it traversed Greenville County on a ridge east of the Enoree River and bisected the route of the future Super Highway.[22] It became known, also, as the Buncombe Road (different from the Buncombe Road in Greenville) because it led to Buncombe County in the North Carolina mountains. Mann Baston of Travelers Rest made similar observations in his book *Early Travel and Accommodations Along the Roads of the Upper Part of Greenville County, South Carolina*. He noted that Native people and animals had used the land for hundreds of years and had determined the best grades, the best places for fording streams and the best routes.[23] The Super Highway, on the other hand, cut a straight swath and bisected the old roads and trails, which had often followed the terrain.

Today, one of the most visible indications of the Native-colonial interactions is a historical marker on the Indian Boundary in Greer erected by the Joyce Scott Chapter of the Daughters of the American Revolution.

Indian Boundary Line. The Boy Scouts are (*left*) William S. Moore and (*right*) Scott Dillard. *Greer Heritage Museum.*

Erected in 1952 near the county line along the Super Highway, it was moved in 2012 to be better protected at the Greer City Park.[24] The new location is even more appropriate, alongside the boundary line at present Line Street. It is also adjacent to the present Greer City Park pond, filled by a historic

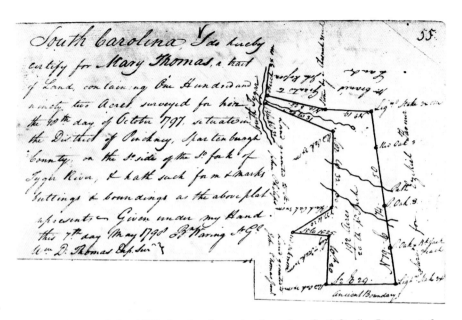

Mary Thomas, land plat, 1797, showing the ancient boundary. *South Carolina Department of Archives and History.*

spring and part of the headwaters of Ward's Creek, which is, in turn, a tributary of the South Tyger River. In Greer, land issued to William Crain (1793), W.D. Thomas (1795) and Mary Thomas (1797) was all bounded at least in part by the Ancient Indian Boundary Line.[25]

The boundary line in many ways sums up Native-colonial contact. It is the story not only of white settlers and their difficulties but also of the Cherokee and "squatters" on their land. Marked once by blazed trees, it is now a line on the map bisecting the Super Highway, a boundary between Spartanburg and Greenville Counties and a noteworthy part of South Carolina history.

Chapter 2

CHICK SPRINGS

G reenville, South Carolina, with its upper piedmont rolling landscape, was at one time known for its springs. Local springs and place names today reveal that history: the Waddy Thompson Spring, Butler Springs, Poinsett Springs, Sulphur Springs on Paris Mountain, Spring Street, Verner Springs, Spring Park Inn in Travelers Rest and "springs" as a popular name for upscale housing or apartment communities today. Numerous small springs existed in the area that became the Super Highway corridor, some with local names, long forgotten. Many were north of the Super Highway, and their streams flowed south into the Enoree, South Tyger or Middle Tyger Rivers, the view of the streams often obscured today by large dirt fills that undergird the Super Highway. There was one exception: Chick Springs was the largest and most celebrated in the area that was to become the unincorporated community of Taylors, South Carolina, historically associated in numerous ways with Greer and today a suburb of Greenville. Sections of Chick Springs Road remaining today are a reminder of a one-hundred-plus-year history of the site—of a natural history of South Carolina's springs and of entrepreneurs who made it into a resort and more. Described by a visitor as "the Saratoga of Greenville," it drew planters from South Carolina and some as far away as Louisiana.[26] Chick Springs in its ensuing history would reflect not only natural history and healing but also social and cultural history—both local and regional—and entrepreneurship.

Chick Springs got its name from its purchaser, Dr. Burwell Chick of Charleston and Newberry, South Carolina, who hunted on the land in the

1830s. Known first as Lick Springs, Dr. Chick's Lick Spring and other names, the 192-acre site came to be known over time as Chick Springs. By tradition, Native Americans valued the spring water for its curative properties and the black earth under the spring for healing "desperate cases of ringworm." In a related tradition, in 1832, two Native Americans from their village along the Enoree River guided Dr. Chick to the springs where deer came to lick the minerals in exposed rocks.[27]

These were "settlement Indians," remnant families of Native Americans—likely Catawba—who had found refuge at times in the area. (The late Taylors historian Jean Martin Flynn suggests that they were Catawba.)[28] These Native peoples likely lived much as local white people and perhaps in log homes, but they settled close to their own to form a community or settlement, all the time keeping some age-old traditions.[29]

Chick Springs' waters were part of a healing tradition of springs such as God's Acre Healing Springs near Blackville, Barnwell County, South Carolina. Governor John Drayton visited the area in 1802 and wrote of a sulphur spring emanating from Paris Mountain. Architect and mapmaker Robert Mills journeyed to what became Chick Springs. He described it as smelling strongly like the "washings of a gun barrel" and, further, that the "beautiful spring bursts and boils up from the earth in a large stream," its waters "of so salubrious a nature that many persons visit them in the autumn for health."[30] The mineral content in the nineteenth century was thought to be largely sulphur and iron, although a 1929 Clemson College analysis showed much more sulphur than iron.[31] Though scientific chemical analysis was not available in the early years of the resort, doctors and others identified the minerals in certain springs by smell, taste, observation or reputation. They knew drinking certain mineral spring water helped certain ailments and that "deep water" springs often contained sulphur, iron or other minerals.[32]

Promoters of springs played on viewing natural scenery, escaping lowland plantations or urban conditions, breathing fresh air and taking water as a cure. It was a "middle landscape," not the city but not wilderness either. Promoters "improved" nature, smoothing its rough edges—essentially "domesticating nature."[33] Part of it was the romantic notion of communing with nature. In resorts like Chick Springs, people found a natural setting—the spring and Lick Creek and a nearby forested area—with the hotel on a hill overlooking a lake, but it was far from a wilderness setting.[34] And the springs were not a cure-all; no doubt many people "took the water" and expected some miracle cure.

Chick Springs spring water. *Photo by Scott Withrow.*

Here Dr. Chick saw a potential to make money, purchased land and opened a summer resort in 1840. In 1842, he advertised "a commodious" sixty-bed hotel.[35] Like Greenville itself, it would be known as a summer resort for people from Charleston and Lowcountry South Carolina, a place where "refinement" was honored. Many in the "planter class" could afford the hotel and spa in its early years, and they came in elegant clothing befitting their social standing. Those who came often formed a kind of summer community or colony, creating two distinct groups in the Chick Springs community— the largely small farmer population and the summer visitors (three groups when enslaved persons or servants were present). Thus, clothes and manners were important to the people at the springs. Historian Thomas Chambers, referring to other springs (and seeming to apply to Chick Springs), wrote, "A trip to the springs was a social statement, an expression of one's class identity."[36] James Bull, a later owner of Chick Springs, advertised in the July 27, 1906 *Union (SC) Times* that there was "always a happy, congenial crowd of the best people around."[37] Visitors to springs developed friends from places in the South or in the nation. It was conspicuous leisure for those who aspired to positions of leadership in the nation.[38] To further illustrate the two distinct groups, it was noted that Chick Springs Hotel had running water and other "luxuries" that many rural people in the area lacked.[39]

It was common for such springs as Chick Springs to serve as a "marriage market" for young men and maidens and widows "inclined to matrimony." For these persons, "drinking the water" was not first on their list. "The main task was to characterize and categorize potential suitors." A Catholic priest, Father O'Connell, who visited Chick Springs each summer (probably because other Catholics visited), wrote that there were fewer invalids visiting Chick Springs than the "gay and youthful in quest of pleasure or matrimonial alliances" and that "invalids were the smallest number among the guests."[40]

Father O'Connell made other comments on Chick Springs in his book *Catholicity in the Carolinas and Georgia: Leaves of History*. Father O'Connell held mass and services at Chick Springs, noted by some observers as the first Catholic mass in the Greenville area, this at a time when, on a Sunday in the 1850s, a Baptist minister from Furman University in Greenville spoke and condemned the dancing at Chick Springs. According to Father O'Connell, the Baptist minister condemned the resort, its people and dancing especially and said that "all at the place were irretrievably lost." At the end, in a place where people usually enjoyed dancing, he had few listeners.[41]

After Dr. Chick's death in 1847, a succession of owners, including Dr. Chick's sons and later South Carolina Lowcountry investors, continued the resort with the addition of billiards, tenpins on the lawn, dances and grand balls, including an 1853 celebration to honor the state's governor, John J. Manning. Its clientele likely changed in the 1880s as middle-class Americans sought places to spend their leisure time—whole families vacationing. But the resort never gained its former status before the Civil War.[42]

Despite the social and cultural differences, some area farmers prospered by selling farm produce, poultry and livestock to the resort (fresh, local food). Landowners saw an increase in land value, and local leaders such as Alfred Taylor provided lumber and bricks for building the resort. Taylor, the namesake of Taylors Station—now the Taylors Community—started out as a hack (stagecoach-like vehicle) driver who brought summer guests from Greenville who had arrived there by railway, worked in the resort's stables and, in 1860, became hotel manager. His knowledge of bridge building and his supervision of the building of a bridge over the Enoree River possibly came from discussions with engineers staying at Chick Springs. Taylor, who was born along what became Main Street in Taylors, lived in the community all his life. He and his family especially tied Chick Springs to the community. Both Alfred and his brother Washington Taylor kept diaries, Washington's the

Alfred Taylor's gravestone. *Photo by Scott Withrow.*

Chick Springs octagonal church. *Taylors First Baptist Church.*

most well known. They wrote of a community where agriculture was a "way of life."[43] Both brothers thought of themselves as farmers.[44]

The Civil War hastened the demise of the first years of the resort. There were no guests after 1861. In 1862, the first hotel burned, and its skeletal ruins lay untouched for twenty-three years until the hotel was rebuilt in 1885. Local historian Jean Martin Flynn observed that if the hotel had not burned, the center of community might have remained at Chick Springs and not shifted up the hill. Important to this shift was the coming of the Airline Railway in 1873, and with it came the name Taylors Station, now the town of Taylors. (The Southern Railway and P&N Railway would come later.) Members of the Chick Springs octagonal church, a wooden structure built in 1864 near the spring, decided also in 1884 to move to Taylors Station and took down the old church. The new church in Taylors became Taylors First Baptist.[45]

In 1885, George Westmoreland, an Atlanta attorney, bought the Chick Springs estate in a series of transactions, with part of the property going for $2,750. He built a small hotel and several cottages, but he sold the company in 1903 to some Greenville businessmen. Prominent among those men was James A. Bull, the name most associated with Chick Springs in the twentieth century.[46] Bull's doctor in Greenville had sent him to Chick Springs for his health, and by 1903, Bull had become the principal stockholder and owner and would become its biggest promoter. He rebuilt the hotel for $45,000 (adding to the original structure), employing carpenters from North Carolina and paying them from a dollar to one and a half dollars a day. Bull traveled to Charleston, Atlanta, Birmingham and New Orleans to promote his property.[47]

CHICK SPRINGS HOTEL, CHICK SPRINGS, NEAR GREENVILLE, S C.

Left: Chick Springs Hotel (Spanish architecture). *Greer Heritage Museum.*

Opposite: Chick Springs advertisement, *Greenville News*, May 29, 1918.

This hotel burned in 1907, and Bull built an even larger hotel of Spanish architecture. Bull, a Greenville grocer known especially for his coffee sales, was quite an entrepreneur and promoter. Newspaper articles and ads from the period again give testimony to the medicinal qualities of the water, "without absolute impurity of any kind," and the resort as a place for "health, rest, and recreation," including tennis, golf and horseback riding. One ad emphasized its superlatives: "Situated in the foothills of the Blue Ridge with 1,300 feet altitude, the nights and days are cool, and there are no mosquitoes!"[48]

In connection to Camp Sevier and World War I, the hotel housed a preparatory military school, Chick Springs Military Academy (1916–17), and its cadets traveled back and forth from the academy to Camp Sevier via the P&N Railway. Again, in connection with the site as a health destination, it became a sanitarium (1919–32), boasting five doctors and a school of nursing.[49] Ads in 1918 emphasized Chick Springs' ties to the military, saying that it connected two of the South's largest army camps (Camp Wadsworth in Spartanburg was only thirty minutes away and Camp Sevier in Greenville was ten minutes away); that it was the "home of army men and families"; that there were military balls; and that it was located on the new electric railway (Piedmont and Northern or P&N) between Spartanburg and Greenville.[50]

Although no known hotel register exists nor is there a complete account of those who came to "take the waters" of Chick Springs, various sources give a picture and some names. Numerous newspapers carried names of people who spent some time at the resort. This was especially true during the World War I years and people—officers and others—associated with Camp Sevier. The *Greenville News* for July 19, 1918, carried the names of many, some military officers for dinner parties and dances and some women who were there for more extended periods of time because their husbands were stationed at Camp Sevier.[51]

By 1927, the water was bottled and sold as Chick Spring Ginger Ale.[52] The ginger ale never became a cult favorite like Blenheim Ginger Ale—still produced today in Blenheim, Marlboro County, South Carolina—but its antique bottles still fetch a worthy price. World War I and the Great Depression took their toll, and the hotel closed and ginger ale bottling ended.[53]

A Chick Springs Company continued, focused on the spring, its mineral water and an adjacent amusement park, described by the *Greenville News* as a "little Coney Island."[54] In a 1935 letter to John A. Bull, U.S. House of Representatives member (Fourth South Carolina District) John McSwain wrote that since President Roosevelt didn't drink mineral water, Bull should send him a "five-gallon demijohn" of Chick Springs water, "securely and hermetically sealed," along with the Clemson College analysis of the water.[55]

In 1925, construction of the National Highway split the property and took the amusement park. After flooding and a backup of sand and silt in the spring, the owner sued the South Carolina Highway Department.[56] The name lived on in Chick Springs Park, with its springhouse, gazebo, dance platform and swimming lake. The lake was large and filled with a sandy base, with the sand shipped in by the boxcar load, and it was fed by Lick Creek. The original lake extended north to a portion taken by construction of the Super Highway, which created a smaller lake. Amazingly, the lake existed for forty-five years, and there are still people in the area who remember swimming in the lake with its sandy bottom. It was open until 1972, when it was closed and drained.[57] Some remember, too, that the Bull family placed a wire fence over the intake from the creek to keep out snakes, but sometimes a small snake would get through, and those on duty would close the pool and use a net to get out the creature.[58] Greer resident Buddy Bowman was fascinated

Chick Springs Hotel

Chick Springs, S. C.

A famous resort in the foothills of the Blue Ridge Mountains on the new Electric Railway between Spartanburg and Greenville. Also connecting two of the South's largest Army Camps—
CAMP SEVIER 10 Minutes. CAMP WADSWORTH 30 Minutes.

Home of Army Men and Families

Mineral Springs. AMERICAN PLAN Truck Farms. Military Balls. Open Air Swimming Pool. Orchestra. 1918 Season opened May 15th.
Under management of Atlantic City Hotel Man.

Left: Chick Springs swimming lake ad, *Greenville News*, May 29, 1918.

Below: Chick Springs today. *Photo by Scott Withrow.*

Opposite: A label for Chick Spring Ginger Ale, circa 1927. *Courtesy of Greenville County Library System, South Carolina Room Archives.*

when his favorite teacher, Miss Margaret Bull (of the Bull family of Chick Springs), once waded into the pool to catch a harmless water snake with her hands.[59] (Miss Bull taught at Victor Elementary in Greer for forty-five years and often worked as a counselor at Camp Burgess Glen.)[60] People in Greer remember swimming afterward in Suttle's Pool, a concrete pool known locally as Suttle's/Suddle's Puddle, a reportedly good pool along the Super Highway that is now the site of a motel.[61]

But the story does not end with the closing of the swimming lake. Various entrepreneurial projects lasted only short periods or did not get off the ground at all. One man stocked the lake with trout for a fishing lake, and some people came fishing, but it did not last. As late as 1989, a local entrepreneur created a recreational gem mine for Chick Springs Park. He had soil shipped from Macon County, North Carolina gem mines to be placed in the old sand bed of the swimming pool. "Miners" stood on clean sand much like the fine sand on the beach and gathered dirt and sand to be put in a sluice to separate out any gems. As with the swimming pool, water came from Lick Creek, originating in a spring itself, its headwaters off St. Mark's Road to the north. Patrons of the mine reportedly found gems—one young girl finding one worth $750—but the mine closed after a successful three years.[62]

The aging Chick Springs Hotel was torn down sometime before 1971 and a house built on its foundation.[63] Today, the spring, springhouse and a gazebo remain adjacent to Lick Creek, both on private property. The seven-acre springhouse site was never developed as a public park, as some envisioned. But Taylors Town Square, a community development organization, is working to change that and to turn the Chick Springs property into a park and a trailhead for an Enoree River trail system.[64] Development of the site is fitting since it was an important part of upstate history, part of the resort era with its emphasis on health and renewal. It was as much a part of local history as it was regional history.

Twentieth-century postcards show an arboretum-like garden of plants on the land surrounding the springhouse. In some photos, dogwood trees in bloom are evident in the background. Today, patches of daffodils, Lenten rose and other flowers bloom in the spring, and on a hillside above the spring, small bushes of rhododendron struggle among low-growing wisteria for existence. Today, too, large oaks and beech trees form the canopy of a site that has captured the imagination of entrepreneurs, nature enthusiasts, health seekers and matrimony-minded people for close to two centuries.

Chapter 3

THE RAILWAYS

Southern and P&N

Before the advent of good roads in the 1920s, railroads played a very important role in the economic success of Greenville and Spartanburg. The two cities had been connected by rail lines for many years before the Super Highway was constructed. The building of the Super Highway paralleled the lines of two established railroads. One was the Southern Railway and the other the Piedmont and Northern (P&N) Railway. In the thirty or so miles between Greenville and Spartanburg, the Super Highway crossed these rail lines at several different points. One of the first major projects in the building of the Super Highway was the construction of twin bridges over the rail lines of the Southern Railway and the P&N Railway near the intersection with the old Camp Road. The section of the Southern Railway between Spartanburg and Greenville was a part of its main line from Washington, D.C., to New Orleans, Louisiana. The P&N Railway provided a heavily used method of transportation for interurban passengers and freight traffic that connected towns such as Greer with the cities of Spartanburg and Greenville. The railroads helped make Spartanburg a hub for commercial expansion. A report of the Railroad Commission in 1940 stated that Spartanburg County ranked first in the state for total value of railroad property.[65]

The Piedmont and Northern Railway was divided into the North Carolina Division and the South Carolina Division. They were never connected. The northernmost end of the South Carolina Division was at

Above: Southern Railway Locomotive 4877 at Spartanburg. *Joseph Hudson Collection.*

Opposite, top: Piedmont and Northern Railway at night. *Greer Heritage Museum.*

Opposite, middle: Former Piedmont and Northern Railway Depot (Greer). *Photo by Scott Withrow.*

Opposite, bottom: Excerpt from *Days and Times Remembered* by Constance Hemphill Dillard. *Courtesy of Ann Dillard Withrow.*

Spartanburg. Prior to the end of World War II and the completion of the Super Highway in 1946, the Piedmont and Northern was very busy with passenger traffic.[66] In 1904, there were only 7 privately owned automobiles in Spartanburg County. In 1940, four years after the work on the Super Highway commenced, there were 23,450 privately owned automobiles in the county.[67] It seems obvious that the development of the Super Highway helped change the mode of transportation for a large number of people traveling between Spartanburg and Greenville. Greer resident Constance Hemphill Dillard wrote in *Days and Times Remembered* about a neighbor with appendicitis who was taken to a Spartanburg hospital on the Piedmont and Northern.[68]

Besides carrying passengers, the Piedmont and Northern delivered thousands of bales of cotton to the numerous mills between Spartanburg and Greenville. Prior to World War II, this section was the most industrialized area in the state.[69] The route of the Piedmont and Northern from Spartanburg to Greenville passed through towns along the Super

P. AND N. TRAIN AT CHICK SPRINGS, NEAR GREENVILLE. S. C.

Claudia. One incident I recall about Mrs. Hughes was the time
she was stricken with appendicitis. Greer still had no hospital.
So Mrs. Hughes had to be taken on a cot to Parker stop, put aboard
the P and N railway and transported to Spartanburg for an operation.

Piedmont and Northern trestle, Taylors, South Carolina. *Photo by Scott Withrow.*

Highway that had textile mills. These towns were Startex, Lyman, Duncan, Greer and Taylors.[70] Greenville had more mills involved in the production of textiles than did any other region and was known as the "Textile Center of the World."[71]

In the 1920s, there was a development that impacted the main cash crop grown in the region between Greenville and Spartanburg. Until the 1920s, the main crop had been cotton. At that time, the boll weevil made its appearance and became a very real threat to cotton production. Farmers in Spartanburg County discovered that the soil in their part of the state was suitable for the growing of peaches. A campaign led by Spartanburg County farm agent Ernest Carnes was established in 1920 in order to spread the word about growing peaches.

The peach industry in the upstate of South Carolina was a success from the very beginning. In 1924, four railroad cars loaded with peaches were shipped to markets in the North. By 1936, the year that construction on the Super Highway began, there were 646 railroad cars of peaches being shipped from farmers in Spartanburg County. In 1938, there were 1,800,000 peach trees planted in Spartanburg. In 1939, the Georgia-Carolina Peach

Dillard Pic Pac peach label. *Courtesy of Ann Dillard Withrow.*

Marketing Board was formed.[72] The growth of the peach industry could be seen along the Super Highway corridor during the 1930s and 1940s. The planting, growing, picking, packing, icing of railroad reefer cars and shipping of peaches all took place along this thirty-mile corridor of concrete. Train crews were kept busy switching railroad cars from June to August each year at Greer, Inman and Spartanburg. Southern Railway had six rail yards devoted to the handling of peaches. The peaches were shipped to such places as Alexandria, Virginia; Memphis, Tennessee; Cincinnati, Ohio; and Louisville, Kentucky.[73]

Growers often trucked the peaches to railway sidings for shipment. They often paid brokers, some out of state, to ship and retail peaches. The Dobson Brothers packing shed near where the Inland Port is located today in Greer was itself a siding, and they moved peaches directly to railroad cars. There was one in downtown Greer and possibly others.

Peach farming families were often excited to get hydrocoolers, which used ice-cold water to cool peaches to keep them from ripening too fast during shipping. In this process, blocks of ice were placed in water in a vat, and the cold water was pumped up and onto baskets of peaches on conveyor belts, cooling them down to almost forty degrees Fahrenheit. Troy H. Cribb at Hayne Yard in Spartanburg operated a commercial hydrocooler for area peach growers.

The railroad cars themselves were interesting. Compartments on either end were filled with ice, and fans, operating from the movement of the train, blew cold air throughout the car.[74]

By the 1950s, better highways led to the shipping of peaches by trucks that could load the fruit at the packing sheds. The Super Highway was improved and widened by the 1960s. In the 1960s, development along the Super

Highway resulted in the disappearance of the once familiar peach orchards between Greenville and Spartanburg.[75] Mac McMillin, whose family owned a peach orchard in Lyman, said this in an article he wrote in 2005 for *TIES* magazine: "The last crop of peaches sold directly to truckers straight from the orchard, with no processing whatsoever. After that last season, my dad had a bulldozer brought in that pushed up all the trees into huge piles where they were burned. Not a single tree was spared. I don't remember the year but I estimate it was 1960 or 1961."[76] Shipping peaches by rail or truck is largely a practice of the past; most are sold today in local markets.

Chapter 4

MILITARY CAMPS

Sevier and Wadsworth

In 1917, after the United States entered World War I, two U.S. Army training camps were established in the upstate of South Carolina: one in Greenville and the other in Spartanburg. Each camp was near the ends of what would be the Super Highway. In Greenville, there was Camp Sevier, which was named for John Sevier, who was an American officer during the Revolutionary War. Sevier fought in the Battle of Kings Mountain (South Carolina) on October 7, 1780. After the American Revolution, Sevier became the first governor of Tennessee. Spartanburg saw the establishment of Camp Wadsworth, which was named for New Yorker James Wadsworth, a brigadier general in the Union army during the Civil War. He was killed at the Battle of the Wilderness in 1864. The main unit to train at Camp Wadsworth was the Twenty-Seventh Division. It was made up primarily of a contingent of soldiers from New York. The first troops arrived at Camp Sevier in July 1917 and were quartered in tents. The camp covered close to two thousand acres. The U.S. War Department rented land from private property owners. The first arrivals at Camp Sevier were put to work clearing large areas of pine forests. The camp hospital was located on property across from where the current Sevier Middle School stands today. The camp had a library. It was a quiet place where soldiers could read books, newspapers and magazines. It was also a good place for the soldiers to write letters home to friends and family. The camp post office handled huge volumes of mail each day. The first soldiers to be assigned to Camp Sevier were from national guard units of North Carolina, Tennessee and South Carolina. They became the nucleus of the Thirtieth Division, which was known as "Old Hickory." After the Thirtieth Division left for France, parts of the Eighty-First (Wildcat) Division trained at Camp Sevier until they, too, left for France. On the day that the armistice was signed to end the Great War, the Twentieth Division was training at the camp. Construction of the camp was under the auspices of J.E. Sirrine and the Gallivan Company of Greenville. The U.S. government officially closed the activities at the camp in April 1919.[77]

After soldiers began to arrive at Camp Sevier in Greenville, one of the first problems that had to be dealt with was the condition of the road between Greenville and the camp. The road was in bad need of repair. The pavement ended about one mile from the camp. The remainder of the route was dirt, and heavy rains caused deep holes and a covering of mud up to nine inches deep. Heavy traffic from Greenville to the camp only made matters worse. Public transportation vehicles were unable to transport the thousands of soldiers who wished to go to or return from Greenville. It was said that even four-wheel-drive trucks became stuck in the quagmire of mud. Many drivers refused to take soldiers any farther than the end of the concrete-paved road. This caused soldiers to walk a mile in the mud to return to camp. A dirt road could not support the heavy traffic between Greenville and Camp Sevier, and camp officers were not happy that soldiers were delayed in returning to camp from Greenville.[78]

Public transportation drivers proposed to raise their fares from twenty-five cents to fifty cents because of the bad road conditions, and as a consequence, the authorities at Camp Sevier threatened to ban any vehicles charging increased fares.[79]

With these problems, many soldiers chose to stay in camp rather than make the effort to find transportation to Greenville. The Piedmont and Northern Railway running between Camp Sevier and Greenville could not keep up with the increased ridership due to the poor conditions of the road to the camp.[80] Within the boundaries of the camp itself, there were different kinds of roads. These included oil (covered) roads, concrete roads and rock-surfaced roads.[81]

In 1917, the U.S. War Department built a new army training camp about three miles west of the city of Spartanburg. It covered approximately two thousand acres and was constructed in a mostly rural and heavily forested area. The Fiske-Carter Company was awarded the contract to build what would become known as Camp Wadsworth. Soldiers were quartered in pyramidal-type tents that could accommodate eight men. The soldiers who

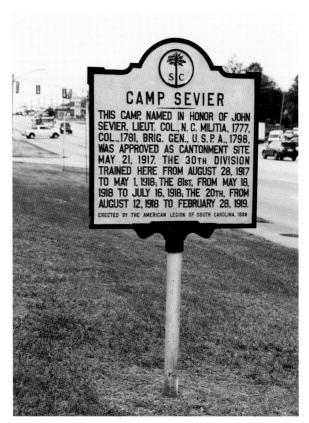

Right: Camp Sevier historical marker. *Photo by Scott Withrow*.

Below: Thirtieth Division uniform. *Military History Center of the Carolinas*.

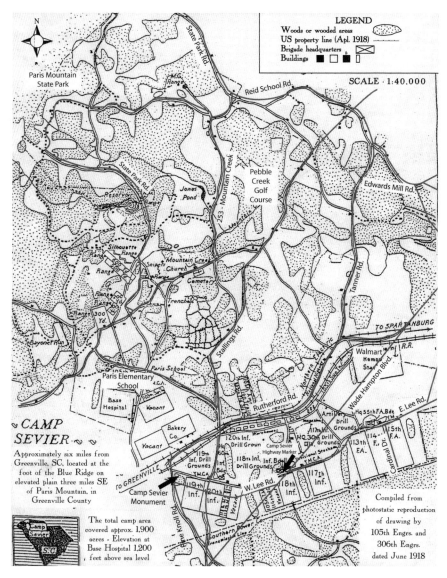

Camp Sevier, South Carolina, United States Army Corps of Engineers. *Greenville County Library System, Main–South Carolina Collection.*

arrived in Spartanburg in 1917 were members of the New York National Guard. They entered service in the United States Army as the Twenty-Seventh Division. The soldiers at Camp Wadsworth trained in a trench system that covered eight miles. The Twenty-Seventh Division may have been given the best training of any American division that participated in

Camp Sevier remount station. *Military History Center of the Carolinas.*

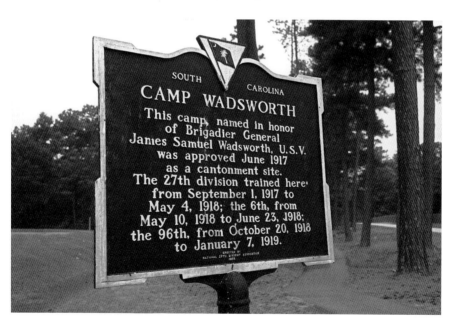

Camp Wadsworth historical marker. *Photo by Scott Withrow.*

Top: World War I trench warfare. *PICRYL.com.*

Bottom: Camp Wadsworth road construction. *Spartanburg County Library Kennedy Room.*

World War I.[82] The Twenty-Seventh Division embarked for France in April 1918, fighting in the major operations of Ypres-Lys, the Somme Offensive and the Defensive Sector.[83]

The road that led from Spartanburg to Camp Wadsworth was dangerous to drive on in 1917. It was full of twists and turns between very steep embankments. There were almost daily accidents due to the many sharp

SNAKE ROAD OR VANDERBILT HIGHWAY BUILT BY THE SOLDIERS, CAMP WADSWORTH, SPARTANBURG, S. C.

Above: Camp Wadsworth road construction. *Spartanburg County Library Kennedy Room.*

Left: Straightening Snake Road, Spartanburg, South Carolina. *Spartanburg County Public Library.*

curves. It became the job of Colonel Cornelius Vanderbilt (from New York) and the Twenty-Second Regiment of Engineers under his command to straighten the "Snake Road" and make it safe for motorists. One major problem that had to be overcome was the shortage of a labor supply to rebuild the winding road to the camp. Convict labor from the city and county of Spartanburg was turned over to Colonel Vanderbilt to assist in road construction. Colonel Vanderbilt did most of the survey work himself, mapping out where curves were to be eliminated. Approximately one hundred convicts from city and county prisons worked along with the army engineers to straighten the winding road from Spartanburg to Camp

49

Wadsworth. Colonel Vanderbilt directed the removal of trees and any obstacles that stood in the way of the work on the road. He supervised the building of four bridges. After a quarry of granite was discovered during the road construction, Colonel Vanderbilt acquired the necessary machinery to crush it. The crushed stone was used to pave the road and also to pave main roads that ran through Camp Wadsworth. As a result of Colonel Vanderbilt's leadership in straightening the Snake Road, the soldiers at Camp Wadsworth as well as the citizens of Spartanburg referred to it as the "Vanderbilt Road," a portion of which still exists.[84]

Chapter 5

THE NATIONAL HIGHWAY

It is not everyday history, but people find it incredible that portions of the Bankhead National Highway remain in Spartanburg, Greenville and other counties. In the Carolinas and Georgia, the Bankhead Highway followed much but not all of a slightly earlier Southern National Highway route centered on an Atlanta-to-Mississippi hub. The Bankhead expanded the route in the east and west to San Diego. In South Carolina, especially, the route pieced together existing roads, but local communities often improved roads in hopes of being on the route.[85] Sometimes, the highway is referred to by both names, but the highway is hereinafter referred to as the National Highway, the first name for portions of the highway and the name more known in South Carolina over time. "Bankhead" was used more in Alabama and Texas and in the West.[86]

The road's route between Spartanburg and Greenville roughly paralleled the later route of the Super Highway. Begun after 1916 and before the U.S. highway numbering system, the National Highway was the nation's second transcontinental highway, after the Lincoln Highway established in the North in 1913. A Greer historical marker reads:

> *The Bankhead National Hwy. Association was formed in 1916 with the goal of creating a transcontinental highway that would run from Washington, D.C. to San Diego, CA. When completed in 1920, it became the second transcontinental highway in the U.S. The National Hwy., also known as the Bankhead Hwy., connected towns across the S.C.*

Upstate. It crossed into S.C. near Blacksburg and passed through Gaffney, Spartanburg, Greer, Greenville, and Anderson. John Hollis Bankhead (1842–1920), a U.S. Senator from Alabama and advocate of the Good Roads Movement, sponsored the Federal Road Aid Act of 1916, which authorized $75 million for road improvement and was the first federal highway funding law. The National Hwy. passed through Greer, following what is now Poinsett St. Later, the Super Hwy. (now Wade Hampton Blvd.) and Interstate 85 would replace the National Hwy. as the main route from Charlotte to Atlanta.[87]

Named after President Abraham Lincoln, the Lincoln Highway connected Times Square in New York City to Philadelphia and then followed old military roads, Indian trails and other established roads across the continent to San Francisco. But the highway was routed through the upper Midwest and across the Sierra Nevada at Donner Pass, which, with its northern location, often made it inaccessible in winter months.[88]

The National Highway, on the other hand, was routed south and skirted the Appalachians before turning west in Georgia through Alabama, Mississippi, Tennessee, Arkansas, Texas, New Mexico and Arizona and ending in San Diego. Touted as the first all-weather coast-to-coast highway, its construction was one of the first instances of federal aid to states for highway construction.[89] Notably, it was routed south of Route 66 in the West.[90]

It was known as the Bankhead Highway, especially in the lower South and Texas, after its chief proponent, Senator John Hollis Bankhead (1842–1920) of Alabama. It was also known as "the Broadway of America," while others refer to it as the "Route 66 of the South" (terms used more in the West).[91] But the real Route 66 has received much of the fame; no John Steinbeck or other writer traveled and wrote about the National Highway to the extent Steinbeck did of Route 66.[92]

Bankhead Highway map. *Courtesy of Steven Varner, Varner's American Roads.*

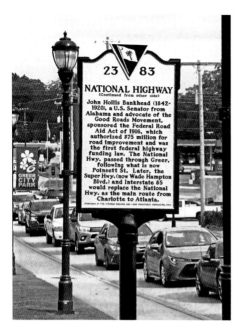

National Highway historical marker. *Photo by Scott Withrow.*

The Good Roads Movement (1870s–1920s), giving the promise of accessibility to travel, spread across the nation, promising to "get the nation out of the mud."[93] Many roads before this time, financed by cities and counties and other local interests, were dirt, muddy and impassable in harsh weather. Travel by horseback (or wagon) was the main mode of travel, and there was no reason to bridge small streams. In short, roads were designed neither for bicyclists nor people driving automobiles. A trip on southern roads was often an adventure. Often, the term "You can't get there from here!" was no joke.[94] A 1909 Good Roads Tour intended to mark a new national highway route traveled from New York to Atlanta. Thirty-eight cars began the trip, some racing and some touring. A hand-painted banner welcomed them to Greer on their way to Greenville, Anderson and Atlanta.[95]

The National Highway had its beginnings in the Good Roads Movement. It had important promoters: its namesake, John Bankhead, and John Asa Rountree. Senator John Bankhead (1842–1920) of Alabama came to support good roads nationwide, especially for farmers who complained of bad farm-to-market roads.[96] In 1916, Bankhead, an ardent New Dealer, sponsored legislation (Federal Aid Road Act of 1916) that first served as a model for federal-state cooperation for building highways. As president of the United States Good Roads Association, he traveled the country to encourage good roads and, for his support, became known as the "Father of Good Roads." His support of a southern route for a national highway led to the creation of the (Bankhead) National Highway.[97] "America," he said, "needs good roads almost as bad as she needs soldiers and guns."[98] Bankhead was likely familiar with Greenville County since his wife, Tallulah James Brockman Bankhead, was born in the Gilder Creek area of the county.[99] (Their granddaughter was Hollywood actress Tallulah Bankhead.)

Left: West Main, Spartanburg, prior to 1903. Courtesy of *Mark Olencki.*

Opposite: The Good Roads Tour through Greer. *Cliff Davenport Collection, Greer Heritage Museum.*

John Asa Rountree (1867–1936) was a Birmingham publisher and advocate for good roads. Like Bankhead, he was active in the Good Roads Movement, and he founded and became the first secretary of the United States Good Roads Association. He shifted much of his attention to the National Highway, and he convinced the U.S. Army to conduct a 1920 convoy over the highway as it had done for the Lincoln Highway the previous year. More than Bankhead, he was a pathfinder, traveling and exploring routes for the Bankhead and other roads. He was the only civilian to participate in the 1920 military convoy on the National Highway.[100]

One other person, Thomas Harris MacDonald (1881–1957), deserves special mention in relationship to the National Highway. Although he was not associated specifically with the National Highway from its start, he became its champion along with other highways "interstate in character." He was appointed commissioner of the U.S. Bureau of Public Roads in 1919, a position he held until 1953. In that position, he brought systematic and scientific study to our system of national roads, and his proposals for interstate highways became the model for the interstate highway system. He deserved the title "father of the nation's highway system."[101] MacDonald epitomized the role of civil engineers and the superiority of technical expertise in development of interstate highways.[102]

The role of boosterism and economic development should not be overlooked. There were different kinds of boosters. Some approached better roads from a national standpoint, but others in the South worked on the local level, hoping to bring capital that had previously gone to New York or other places. To some, economic development became a panacea for the problems of the South.[103]

Not everyone was a promoter; some saw the National Highway as a road for the wealthy who could afford to travel long distances. Farmers, for example, were interested in farm-to-market roads and rural free delivery.[104] To agrarians such as Andrew Nelson Lytle of Vanderbilt University, "Good road programs drive like a flying wedge and split the heart of provincialism—which prefers religion to science, handicrafts to technology, the inertia of the fields to the acceleration of industry, and leisure to nervous prostration."[105] Many before World War I saw the National Highway as class legislation, "chiefly for the benefit of more fortunate neighbors who owned and drove their own motor cars."[106] Southern farmers often opposed new roads for other reasons. Since colonial times, farmers in the South had paid their taxes by doing required maintenance on a section of road near their homes for a number of days each year. The work was done at local government levels. The change to state and federal responsibility created a system of taxation for road improvements. Why change an age-old tradition, many cash-strapped farmers asked?[107] Easterners (those of the Middle Atlantic and New England states) were often opposed to federal aid since they would have to pay taxes for roads they thought would be built largely in the South and West.[108]

Long-distance roads like the National Highway were seen by some as part of the Progressive Era but, in fact, evolved to become a part of boosterism that favored the urban middle class who could afford cars. To officials in some states, it meant federal competition with state road-building interests. The vision moved well beyond the farm-to-market roads advocated by farmers and benefitted urban middle-class Americans and business interests. Alabama senator "Cotton Tom" Heflin, in a Senate committee hearing, scolded what he called "automobilists" as "people who gallivant around the country for joy riding" instead of more practical concerns—"producing the wealth of the nation" (farming or business or rural free mail delivery). Heflin advocated "improved" roads," not new, long-distance interstate highways.[109] There is irony in the fact that he lost his last Senate election to roads advocate John H. Bankhead.[110]

Notably, South Carolina at first received no federal aid for the National Highway because it had no state highway department with which to coordinate federal funds. A March 30, 1916 *Greenville News* article emphasized South Carolina's "backwardness" in building public roads and reported that it was one of five states that lagged behind. The article ended with an encouraging note: "South Carolina is giving the question of a State highway department serious consideration."[111] According to John Hammond Moore in *The South Carolina Highway Department, 1917–1987*, many South Carolinians were suspicious of state government organizations after Ben Tillman's (1847–1918) corrupt state plan to control liquor sales. This suspicion extended to such organizations as the South Carolina State Highway Commission, which was established in 1917 to take advantage of matching federal funds under the Federal Roads Act of 1916. Fears of corruption, Lowcountry versus upcountry issues, personality clashes and World War I led to "growing pains" for the commission.[112]

Others, with national defense in mind, saw the National Highway as a military road. There are some short registers of those who traveled the highway, but none as we know with the stature of a young Dwight D. Eisenhower, who traveled the Lincoln Highway in a military convoy in 1919, which, with his later introduction to Germany's Autobahn, led to his support of interstate highways.[113]

The military was involved in another way. According to local historian Don Koonce, soldiers at Camp Sevier paved the highway from Greenville to Camp Sevier. The camp and the 100,000 soldiers who trained there were significant to the early growth of Greenville. The Camp Sevier section, now part of Rutherford Road, was the first paved road in Greenville County.[114]

Good roads such as the National Highway created a new kind of public place, the American roadside, where local people set up businesses to serve travelers, which, in turn, led to a distinctive roadside architecture. With it came "filling stations," followed by tourist camps—the forerunners of motels—and, with them, a "new, free-wheeling mercantile logic" of doing business.[115] Northerners traveled the South sometimes for the first time, thinking of the area as "a land of perpetual sunshine" where people were laid-back—a place to relax.[116]

You best get a good sense of the National Highway history on Main Street in Taylors and Highway 290 from Greer, via Duncan and Lyman, to the Wellford area. In Taylors, the Taylors School, its cannery building, numerous old storefronts and service stations, some unused at this writing, remain along the route. In Taylors also, the railroad (P&N Railway and trestle), Chick Springs history, the textile era (Southern Bleachery and Piedmont Print Works), an early hardware store, a school, churches, old homes and what was once the National Highway converge to offer a feeling of an earlier time. Driving the highway in this area has the feel of concrete and expansion joints, covered over by layers of asphalt over the years.

In Spartanburg County, the National Highway was first routed from Duncan via parts of Reidville Road to Spartanburg. It was later straightened via Lyman and Wellford to Spartanburg. Lyman is distinguished by its mill village, its former mill site (Lyman Printing and Finishing and its predecessor, Pacific Mills) and its public concrete-lined spring on the edge of town near the

A service station along the National Highway, Taylors. *Photo by Scott Withrow.*

Middle Tyger River. Its renovated mill houses, framed in part with cypress, now are a complement to the community. It recalls a time when a millworker in Lyman could catch the P&N to Greer and watch a movie complete with popcorn and a drink for twenty-five cents. For some, the National Highway (later known as the Spartanburg Highway) and the P&N summon up more memories than the Super Highway.[117] Pacific Mills, based in Boston, built the original Lyman mill facility in 1924. It was a model mill village with 375 millhouses, parks and recreational facilities, churches and a library. The mill was known for its high-quality sheets.[118]

The road from Lyman to Wellford gives a feeling of the original highway with old service stations—including Red Hill Hot Dogs (the building dates to the least the 1930s, and the imprint on a concrete base indicates round gas pumps)—and the former Tucapau-Startex Greyhound bus stop.[119] Florence Chapel United Methodist Church (est. 1883) is located today near the site of Sunny Graded School and the Florence Chapel High School, the African American high school before Byrnes High School was desegregated. The name "Florence Chapel" (for the church and school) apparently came from Florence Moore of Nazareth Presbyterian Church, who, with other members of her family, donated land for the church and taught children in the church community to read. Florence Chapel Middle School, a modern Spartanburg County school, honors the original name and school.[120]

A 1918 map of Camp Wadsworth shows the Old and New National Road, originally routed to the south as part of the Reidville Road. Pictured on the map is the New Greenville Road, passing through camp to continue as Vanderbilt Road (after the camp commander), itself the newly straightened Snake Road. After Camp Wadsworth, it would become the National Highway and the approximate route of the later Highway 29 (the Super Highway). This portion passed Friendship Baptist Church (African American, organized 1876), shown on the map in the midst of camp.[121] Church members worshiped in a tent until 1918 rather than in their church, which was used as a synagogue for Jewish soldiers from New York and a camp library. The church itself was eventually torn down and the boards hauled away, but the cemetery remains today just off Highway 29. Local historians believe the cemetery is the only site remaining in this rapidly urbanizing area that predates Camp Wadsworth.[122] Local historian Susan Thoms has written that oral history indicates that some Camp Wadsworth soldiers are buried in a mass grave in the Friendship Cemetery.[123]

Vanderbilt, as part of the National Highway, continued to form Main Street on to Morgan Square. Spartanburg was considered key to the

Lyman Spring(s). *Photo by Scott Withrow.*

An aerial view of Pacific Mills. *"Days at Pacific Mills: A Lyman Group" (Facebook).*

Red Hill Hot Dogs. *Photo by Scott Withrow.*

highway, a city where the National Highway, the Black Bear Trail and the Appalachian Highway would intersect. (The last two didn't seem to have strong promotion in Spartanburg or elsewhere; theirs are road designations seldom, if ever, heard today.) The city touted its nearness to historic Revolutionary War battlefields such as Cowpens and Kings Mountain.[124]

In Greer, the National Highway became Emma and Hill Streets and, today, Poinsett Street. Homes and some store buildings go back to its early years. Waters Grocery, later Poulson's Grocery (and meat market), occupied the same building. In more recent years, it was an antique store, and today, it has been repurposed even again. Nearby, a modern restaurant, The Clock, accounts for a business long established in Greer. Ponder's Ice Cream also stood later along the historic highway. When Greer was a farming center, a guano (fertilizer) company stood near the corner of Highway 290 and Line Street.

Change has occurred, and some distinctive buildings are gone. These include the P&N Depot in Taylors (Taylors Station) and numerous storefront buildings in Taylors. Perhaps one of the biggest loses was the octagonal, wooden Chick Springs Baptist Church, founded in 1864 during the height of the Civil War and dismantled after the church congregation moved to Taylors Station to establish what became Taylors First Baptist Church.[125]

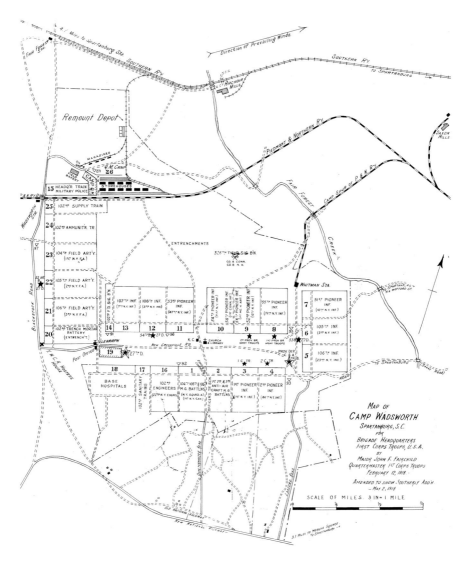

Camp Wadsworth map. *Spartanburg County Library, Kennedy Room.*

Had it remained, Greenville County could have boasted two octagonal churches, the other the brick McBee Chapel in Conestee.

Important to Taylors, too, is the Taylors Mill. Starting as a textile mill in 1924 adjacent to the National Highway, it evolved to become Southern Bleachery and Print Works. Its appearance was described as campus-like with homes, stores, churches, schools and even tennis courts and a nine-hole golf course. Like other area industries, it supported the war effort in World

Left: Emma Street, Greer. *Greer Heritage Museum.*

Opposite: Taylors Mill superintendent's house and historical marker. *Photo by Scott Withrow.*

War II. It survived the Great Depression and World War II, but it could not survive globalization and closed in 1965, its homes auctioned. Due to the vision of Kenneth and Ruby Loftis Walker and others, the mill site has become a place for artists, craftspeople and local restaurants and is also now a meeting venue.[126]

It is enjoyable to travel the National Highway route and distinguish the old parts, those buildings and objects tied to an earlier era—to identify a cottage once part of Chick Springs or an old bridge abutment at the Enoree or Taylors' repurposed mill. It is refreshing to know that the National Highway linked portions of earlier roads—Indian trails, rural routes and the Spanish Trail in the Southwest—and also old trails and rural roads in the Greenville-Spartanburg area, such as Chick Springs and other roads. Like explorers of old, the newly formed Bankhead National Highway Association sent out "pathfinders" to map the new "national auto trail."

In Taylors, it is easy to imagine the 1920 military convoy that traveled the highway when participants motored over portions of the historic highway all the way from D.C. to San Diego. Colonel John F. Franklin, a West Point graduate who had fought with General Pershing against Pancho Villa in Mexico, led the original convoy, which included fifty vehicles, 32 officers and 160 enlisted men and came just after the 1919 Lincoln Highway convoy in which Eisenhower participated. General Pershing himself wasn't part of the second convoy, but he played a part; his Pershing Map was the first blueprint of a national highway system. The convoy began from Zero Milestone near the White House and moved south.[127]

J.A. Rountree, the highway promotor, seemed to be the only civilian on the convoy and kept a bare-bones journal. On June 26, the convoy "left Blacksburg, passed through Spartansburg [*sic*] and Greer, arriving at

Greenville at 6:00, having traveled 71 miles." According to Rountree's notes, it was day twelve of the convoy.[128] South Carolina seemed easy compared to rain on approaching Memphis, mud along the Mississippi and a sandstorm in the West.[129] The convoy members received food and southern hospitality wherever they traveled. Rountree, field director of the motor transport corps, and Lieutenant John Franklin praised the Greenville County portion of the National Highway as "by far the best yet travelled." According to Rountree, the greatest and only trouble was southern hospitality: "The good people along the highway, at every point, stop us, entertain us, feed us, and, incidentally, detain us."[130]

The original convoy had as its purpose the promotion of good roads for both commerce and military transportation. In appreciation of the original convoy, a military group in 2015 reenacted the entire trip. Fifty restored jeeps, trucks and motorcycles made the trip, lasting a month at thirty miles per hour. Leaving Washington, D.C., on Saturday, September 19, 2015, the reenactors followed the journal kept by John Asa Rountree.[131] The convoy was sponsored by the Spirit of '45 organization, the vehicles themselves privately owned and affiliated with the Military Vehicle Preservation Association. After lunch, the vehicle procession left Spartanburg and traveled to Greenville by Highway 29, arriving at the old K-Mart, Church Street, at 3:45 p.m. Many participants were retired from the military, and many dressed the part, making the convoy that much

Convoy reenactment sponsored by Spirit of '45 organization. *Tom Taylor, Random Connections.*

more authentic. World War II veterans and others came to meet those in the convoy and reminisce.[132]

One portion of the National Highway appears more modern today and simply a bypass for the Super Highway. Those who look for old roads and expansion joints often miss Rutherford Road. Though its intersection with the Super Highway has changed, it follows the original route for the most part. Its history goes back to Camp Sevier, when soldiers helped construct the National Highway.[133]

One of the most important burials along this portion of the highway at St. Matthews United Methodist Church is that of Reverend James R. Rosemond (1820–1902), who established the first African American Methodist church in upstate South Carolina in 1865. "Father" Rosemond, as he was known, went on to establish fifty Methodist churches, stretching from Oconee to York County.[134] This included Spartanburg's Silver Hill United Methodist Church, less than a mile from the Super Highway.[135]

One of the National Highway's first businesses was Greenville Nursery, located near the former Lowe's Hardware and the P&N Railway along today's Rutherford Road. Commissioned in 1911 with an office in Greenville, it started with a capital stock of $10,000.[136] From all accounts, it did a thriving business from its opening along the National Highway by 1920,

Above: Bankhead Highway reenactment patch. *Courtesy of Tom Taylor, Random Connections.*

Left: Reverend James Rosemond monument. *Photo by Scott Withrow.*

advertising its location as on the National Highway beyond Camp Sevier.[137] A 1924 ad also placed it along the National Highway and indicated it was accessible to the P&N Railway. It offered conifers, roses, evergreens, fruit trees and shrubs for sale.[138] Also by 1924, the *Greenville News* regarded it as an important institution for Greenville, with eighty acres of nursery stock and eighteen employees.[139] By 1945, the nursery was out of business, selling out to Taylors Nursery. Taylors Nursery, too, later closed, and little, if any, traces remain of the nursery site today, not far from the juncture of Rutherford Road and the Super Highway.

Other industries were connected to textiles. Among these, Steel Heddle stands out.[140] Steel Heddle, a Philadelphia company, made heddles for the textile industry. (According to Merriam-Webster, a heddle is "one of the sets of parallel cords or wires that with their mounting compose the harness used to guide warp threads in a loom.")[141] The move was to establish a sales office in Greenville, home to eleven textile mills as early as 1912. In response to Greenville mill owners, Steel Heddle moved its manufacturing operations to Greenville around 1923. By 1930, the company had also started making shuttles for looms. In 1949, it asked in a newspaper ad for local farmers to supply dogwood logs (shuttles were made of very hard, dense wood) for shuttles since their business was booming.[142]

During World War II, due to the demand for manufacture of military cloth, the textile industry boomed. Steel Heddle, in response, built a larger plant on fifty acres along the National Highway. It became one of Greenville County's largest employers. In 2001, with the declining textile industry, Steel Heddle filed for bankruptcy. Importantly, Steel Heddle stood on land that was once part of World War I Camp Sevier. Today, the original plant still stands and is now operated as Heddle Hill, "a place for artisans, entrepreneurs, creatives, and collaborators to thrive…with workspaces, shops, and entertainment."[143]

Many residents of Greenville worked there. Fred Faber, in an interview the *Greenville News*, spoke of working at the plant in the 1970s when Rutherford Road was two lanes and employees parked in a dirt parking area between the road and railroad. He said that the benefits and pay were good and it was the best place to work in Greenville over a period of twenty years.[144]

Just as important as Steel Heddle was Southern Worsted Manufacturing and textile mill village, also along the National Highway's Rutherford Road section. Southern Worsted was capitalized in 1923 not long after construction of the highway. It was a subsidiary at least at first of the Waterloo Textile Company of New York. Like that of Steel Heddle, it is the story of textile manufacturers moving south to an area conducive to textile manufacturing, with "excellent water supply and railroad facilities." It was to be supplied with the most modern machinery for "spinning, weaving, dyeing, and finishing worsted fabrics." Bennette Eugene Geer, its first president, was involved in textile manufacturing in Greenville County. He was also affiliated with industrialist James B. Duke and was director of the P&N Railway.[145]

Southern Worsted was advertised as the first woolen mill of its kind in the South, with claims that "Greenville men will soon be wearing home-made suits." "Home-made suits" referred to the fact that Southern Worsted sold woolen cloth to be made into Hart, Schaffner and Marx men's suits. The mill, built on land once part of Camp Sevier, was advertised as the only "modern" woolen spinning and weaving plant in the South.[146] In 1940, Southern Worsted helped the war effort by manufacturing "light serge" cloth by contract with the U.S. Army.[147] The company emphasized that it was not a cotton cloth manufacturing facility, although it was situated in an area of many cotton mills.

Like many cotton mills, Southern Worsted built millhouses—at least eighty-four—creating a mill village for workers.[148] Minter Homes of Greenville was awarded a contract for the mill village at a cost of $135,000.[149] Minter Homes, originally operating out of Huntington, West Virginia, moved to the

Southern Worsted Mill. *Arthur Phillips.*

South to take advantage of mill village sales. Emulating Sears-Roebuck, it offered house catalogues and precut materials for each house style.[150] For its manufacturing facility and warehouse, it bought property along the National Highway on what was once part of Camp Sevier.[151]

Mike Reynolds, who grew up in the Southern Worsted Mill village, recalls the community. He remembers 105 millhouses. He and others played in the creeks adjacent to the property. Important to the village was the mill store, near the present gas pumps at Ingles off Stallings Road. The village was behind and then the mill—all adjacent to the P&N Railway. When developers created Pebble Creek (homes and golf course), the Southern Worsted site had not come up for sale. Later, part of the land was purchased and developed. One business stands out to Mike Reynolds—S.B. Fleming Grocery and Cities Service Station in the vicinity of the National Highway and Mill Street. It was a combination hardware, grocery and restaurant, as well as a service station.[152] Fleming Grocery was advertised as located in Paris, South Carolina.[153] Almost nothing remains of the mill and village, torn down years ago. The name "Pebble Creek" seems to be the invention of the company, which developed land for nearby homes and a golf course. The creeks there are tributaries of Mountain Creek, flowing from Paris Mountain and entering the Enoree River near Taylors. Likely, residents— especially children—had local names for creeks, now forgotten.

Like many mill villages, Southern Worsted had its places of worship. For Southern Worsted, it was Southern Worsted Baptist Church, which was organized on December 7, 1924, with fourteen charter members. In 1925, services were held in a government building at Camp Sevier. Members held a service on Easter 1934 in a new church along Rutherford Road (the National Highway).[154] Mike Reynolds describes the church in 1985 as a small white wooden structure with a steeple and inexpensive stained-glass windows. The steeple still exists, now on a different church in the area.[155] Pebble Creek Baptist Church on Reid School Road has its roots in Southern Worsted Church. Longtime member Jeff Mace says that Pebble Creek held its first service the second Sunday of January 1974. A snowstorm prevented having a service on the first Sunday.[156]

The National Highway was home to two hospitals during its early years: the first Shriners Children's Hospital and the Hopewell Tuberculosis Hospital. The original Shriners Children's Hospital, built in 1926, remained at the corner of the National Highway and Pleasantburg Drive for sixty-two years before it moved to new facilities in 1989.[157] The fine-looking building has been repurposed for a nursing facility. Today's Herdklotz Park, on a hillside

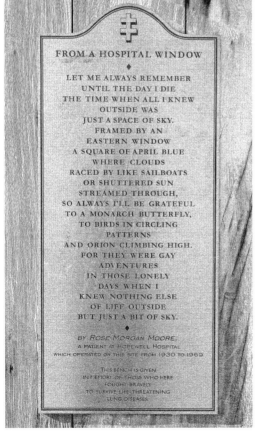

Above: Fleming's Grocery and Service Station. *Courtesy of Janet Fleming-Smith.*

Left: Tuberculosis hospital poem by Rose Morgan Moore. *Photo by Scott Withrow.*

FROM A HOSPITAL WINDOW

LET ME ALWAYS REMEMBER
UNTIL THE DAY I DIE
THE TIME WHEN ALL I KNEW
OUTSIDE WAS
JUST A SPACE OF SKY.
FRAMED BY AN
EASTERN WINDOW
A SQUARE OF APRIL BLUE
WHERE CLOUDS
RACED BY LIKE SAILBOATS
OR SHUTTERED SUN
STREAMED THROUGH,
SO ALWAYS I'LL BE GRATEFUL
TO A MONARCH BUTTERFLY,
TO BIRDS IN CIRCLING
PATTERNS
AND ORION CLIMBING HIGH.
FOR THEY WERE GAY
ADVENTURES
IN THOSE LONELY
DAYS WHEN I
KNEW NOTHING ELSE
OF LIFE OUTSIDE
BUT JUST A BIT OF SKY.

BY ROSE MORGAN MOORE,
A PATIENT AT HOPEWELL HOSPITAL
WHICH OPERATED ON THIS SITE FROM 1930 TO 1969

THIS BENCH IS GIVEN
IN MEMORY OF THOSE WHO HERE
FOUGHT BRAVELY
TO SURVIVE LIFE-THREATENING
LUNG DISEASES

overlooking Rutherford Road (the National Highway), was the site of the Hopewell Tuberculosis Sanitorium, nationally acclaimed for its treatment of tuberculosis patients. Stone remnants of the root cellar and interpretative signage give information on the sanitorium's history.[158]

The National Highway is, in many ways, a lost highway, originally pieced together from rural roads and city streets, when people drove Model Ts and there were few garages and gas stations and motor courts—a time when rain could turn the road into a mud puddle. It is now a jumble of different highway names and numbers, but in places, it is a distinct route often roughly parallel to the Super Highway.[159] Like its markings—yellow, white and black paint on telephone poles in the Greenville area—it is lost to the traveling public.[160] It goes back to days when young people played the game of counting car models or out-of-state license plates in the summer. The National Highway was a humble road, not as exciting as Route 66, but more like the roads traveled in William Least Heat-Moon's *Blue Highways*. It was a journey into the early mind of America.[161]

PART II

THE SUPER HIGHWAY

Chapter 6

BUILDING THE SUPER HIGHWAY

Its Early Years

Superhighways made big news across the nation in the mid-1930s, predating the modern interstate highway system. They were supposed to be straighter, faster, safer—even accident free, according to some—some with little side-road access, all more economical, often "townless highways," much like those in Germany.[162] The Greater Pittsburgh Chamber of Commerce suggested that superhighways would combine the speed of airplanes and the safety of railroads, with no need for speed limits.[163] President Franklin D. Roosevelt was a strong proponent, especially because of the jobs created in building the highways to lift the nation out of the Great Depression. From the start, national and local boosters envisioned superhighways as toll roads, able to pay for themselves. Tom Lewis, author of *Divided Highways*, writes, "Franklin Roosevelt's letters, memoranda, and actions make it clear that he took almost as much enjoyment in planning the construction of roads as he did in driving on them."[164] Conservatives (especially old-guard Republicans), on the other hand, objected to taxes and expanded government powers. There is irony in the fact that moderate Republican President Dwight D. Eisenhower, who had earlier spoken out against "excessive taxation" and "ceaseless expansion" of the federal government, became the father of the Interstate Highway System.[165] Superhighways became associated in time with the Interstate Highway System.

The state and national political maneuverings are not all clear, but due in part to upstate influence and the work of the Greenville Chamber of Commerce, Greenville was selected as the starting point for a superhighway in the South Carolina upstate.[166] Originally, *the* Super Highway (hereinafter written as two words with the first letters capitalized, as it became known in upstate South Carolina) was to be built only to the Taylors community, about seven miles to Greenville's east, but eventually pressure from Spartanburg interests extended it to that city.[167] As news got out, other towns and communities in between envisioned a superhighway (the Super Highway) coming to their locale. Landowners were encouraged to donate land to the project since the highway was said to benefit them.[168]

But the upstate Super Highway was never a toll road and was never a true freeway with limited access—never meeting the exact definition of a superhighway. At first it could be termed a townless highway, with few, if any, traffic lights from Greenville to Spartanburg.[169] It did not take long for businesses and houses to move along the highway, and it quickly became urbanized. Over time, it also became overcrowded, replacing other overcrowded roads. It became a strip of businesses, much like a linear town without a center.[170] To people in the upstate and in nearby North Carolina, the Pennsylvania Turnpike was not the first superhighway as some have written; it was the Super Highway of upstate South Carolina. It was to be the widest highway in the Carolinas.[171]

The Super Highway and its corridor contain a multifaceted history of moonshine and law enforcement, of fast-food restaurants and automobile dealers and of drive-in theaters and recreation.[172] For some, during the '60s especially, it was a virtual curb-hopping, restaurant-cruising *American Graffiti* lifestyle. But the highway was much more over time—taking people to work or to worship, for dinner or entertainment or various other reasons for travel.

On May 3, 1936, the South Carolina State Highway Department took the first steps toward the construction of a superhighway between Greenville and Spartanburg. It published advertisements asking for bids on the grading of 2.8 miles beginning at Greenville. This was under the supervision of Ben M. Sawyer, who was the chief highway commissioner for South Carolina. The bids for the Super Highway were opened at the Jefferson Hotel located in Columbia and announced on May 20, 1936. Chief commissioner Sawyer estimated that the initial costs of the first leg of the Super Highway project would cost approximately $135,000. After review of all the bids, the low bid was announced as being $134,174. The winning bid, made by E.W. Grannis of Fayetteville, North Carolina, was for the first 2.6 miles of the Super Highway beginning in Greenville.[173] Various estimates in 1936 indicated that the total cost of the Super Highway between Greenville and Spartanburg would be between $1,000,000 and $2,000,000.[174]

SUPER HIGHWAY CONTRACTORS

E.W. Grannis Construction Company

E.W. Grannis, a contractor from Fayetteville, North Carolina, was given the contract to grade the first stretch of the Super Highway in 1936. This was the section from Bennett Street in Greenville to a point 2.8 miles from the city.[175] The bid for the project was $134,174 and involved the heaviest grading job ever attempted up to that time.[176] It involved cutting down hills and filling in low spots to reduce grades, as well as the construction of structures for drainage.[177]

Grannis was also awarded a contract for the grading of the second section of the Super Highway. This involved grading from near Brushy Creek to the Greenville Nursery located along the Southern Railway's north–south line. This work included excavation of over 140,000 cubic yards of earth, pressure jetting of embankments, cement work and the laying of concrete pipes for culverts.[178]

H.E. Wolfe Construction Company

The H.E. Wolfe Construction Company of St. Augustine, Florida, was responsible for earth grading and surfacing part of the Super Highway in 1938. The company worked on the section of the dual highway from east of Frye's Creek to the outskirts of Lyman in Spartanburg County. The H.E. Wolfe Construction Company's bid for the project was $176,306.[179]

The owner of the company was Herbert Edward Wolfe, a native of Goodlettsville, Tennessee. Wolfe moved to St. Augustine during World War I and lived there until his death. He started his road construction company in 1923. The H.E. Wolfe Construction Company did road work in Mississippi, Alabama, Georgia, Tennessee, Florida and South Carolina. Besides owning a construction company, Wolfe was a farmer, banker and mayor of St. Augustine (1947–48). He also served on the National Highway Safety Commission under President Eisenhower in the 1950s and was very involved with historic preservation in St. Augustine.[180]

W.F. Bowe Construction Company

The last section of the Super Highway to be paved was done in 1946. It was the eight-mile section of the dual lane between Greer and Lyman. A shortage of materials during World War II had delayed the completion of the Super Highway. The first paving of this last stretch was done by W.F. Bowe Construction Company of Augusta, Georgia.[181]

William F. Bowe built numerous roads in the Southeast. During World War II, his company built concrete aprons and runways for airplane fields in South Carolina and Georgia. Bowe took over ownership of the construction company when his father, R.J. Bowe, passed away in 1893. The R.J. Bowe and Son Construction Company was responsible for doing the brickwork for the state capitol of Georgia, in Atlanta, in 1886.[182]

GRADING FOR THE SUPER Highway from Greenville to Spartanburg began in 1936, surfacing began in 1938 and the highway was completed in 1946, the length of time reflecting delays due to World War II.[183] Jobs were provided for about one hundred men in the initial link of the project. The cost for labor was estimated at about $63,000. The contracting company, E.W. Grannis, was given 250 working days to complete the project.[184]

The completed road between Greenville and Spartanburg would be eighty feet wide. There were to be two separate lanes of pavement for traffic. Each lane would be twenty feet wide with ten-foot shoulders. An earthen lane twenty feet wide would be in the center of the dual lanes. The work on the Super Highway between Greenville and Spartanburg was to be the first of its kind constructed in South Carolina.[185] The old route between Greenville and Spartanburg was the heaviest traveled section of road in South Carolina at the time.

The work on the Super Highway was to begin at the intersection of the Greenville city limits and Bennett Street. The first section would be extended eastward from Greenville for about 2.6 miles. Future work on the Super Highway was planned to extend it to the location of Route 29, which was at a point just to the southwest of Taylors at the time.[186]

From downtown Spartanburg to near downtown Greenville, the highway was twenty-seven and a half miles long. According to the *Greenville News*, at its construction it was "the longest dual lane pavement in the South," the "finest of its type in the country" and "one of the most beautified in this area."[187]

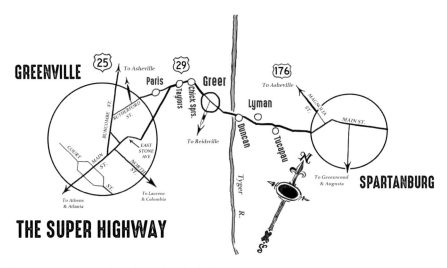

The Super Highway. *Map designed by Sarah McFeely.*

Chambers of commerce and business interests in Spartanburg, Greenville, Greer and other towns and communities saw the road as an economic boom, and politicians campaigned on their support of the road.[188] The existing route through Greer was too crowded, often described as a bottleneck before the Super Highway and especially before completion of the last section.[189] Some wanted it to come through downtown Greer, but if it followed the National Highway route, it would have necessitated that some buildings—still standing today near Poinsett and Trade Streets—would have been torn down. Whatever the route, the highway was to serve as a farm-to-market road and handle much more traffic than existing roads. Newspapers carried articles on how safe the road would be in contrast to two-lane roads.[190]

A vivid memory of those still living who witnessed the construction of the road as children was all the gigantic machinery and the exciting dirt-moving.[191] But persons who remember the construction had to have lived close to it. Rural individuals still living who lived what today we consider "in the area" were often tied to the home and farm and were not aware of all the construction. Someone today who remembers the roadbuilding would be in their eighties or nineties. There are people who might better remember the last industries near or along the Super Highway, such as Pacific Mills at Lyman and the well-built houses in the mill village.[192]

Photos of the construction show surveying, grading, bridge-building (rivers such as the South Tyger, Middle Tyger, North Tyger and Enoree had to be spanned), putting in drainage culverts, road-building machinery, large drainage pipes, grass being sowed, the roadbed being formed and lots of dirt being moved. Photos of the just completed road show a large grassy median (some with the grass just sowed and not well established) and a durable cement road with expansion joints giving a rhythmic beat in driving over them—too rhythmic for some, who grew sleepy driving home from a textile work shift.[193]

The route cut across the landscape in the piedmont (hill country). Securing land for the right of way came first, followed by clearing and grubbing, since in most places it was a new road with no existing path. Early aerial photos show a straight road (in contrast to the curves in more historic roads). This was a modern road for its day, planned by road-building engineers and made with modern machinery (at the time) that cut across or paralleled early roads, some of which originated as Indian trails or wagon roads. Some road elevation gain could not be avoided (there were certain uphill and downhill sections), but the road builders excavated land to make the road as level as possible. This included cuts and fills. Cuts were made through ridges, the latter usually running north to south at a right angle to the highway.

Newly completed Super Highway. *South Carolina Department of Archives and History.*

These ridges appear today as folds in the landscape as drivers look into the distance. From Greer toward Greenville, Burgess Hills will at places stand out in the distance, and farther, Paris Mountain does the same.

Between the folds or ridges (and in the small valleys), small streams usually entered branches of the Tyger or Enoree Rivers at a right angle, flowing generally from north to south. Huge pipes or concrete culverts were installed for these streams, many originating in long-forgotten springs not far north of the Super Highway. Subsequent grading for shopping center parking lots changed the dynamics of the water flow (hydrology) entering the Enoree and branches of the Tyger. The road was constructed using standardized engineering without a large study of any environmental effect—erosion, sedimentation and soil compaction—or archaeology. (Identifying the exact site of the early Hampton family home and family cemetery is problematic because of subsequent widening of the highway. Likewise, no one did a thorough archaeological study of Native American use of the land for hunting or temporary camping.) The rolling, folded nature of the landscape is reflected in the name of Trucker's Hill, the section east of Greer at the South Tyger River (and later the local landmark Tab's Flea Market). Truck drivers got up speed going downhill to make the uphill portion. By all accounts, Ed Mabry and other law enforcement

Super Highway construction. *South Carolina Department of Archives and History.*

officers understood and refrained from giving traffic tickets to truckers speeding down the hill.[194]

South Carolina Department of Archives and History records make numerous mentions of such landmarks as the Greenville Nursery and Chick Springs in Taylors, the Super Highway taking part of the latter.[195] The Greenville Nursery was chartered in 1911 and was seven miles from Greenville. It faced the National Highway and the Piedmont and Northern Railway. The P&N Railway made a stop at the nursery, which covered

Opposite, top: Super Highway construction. *South Carolina Department of Archives and History.*

Opposite, bottom: Burgess Hills (which today looks like a small mountain from Highway 29). *Photo by Scott Withrow.*

Above: Installation of culverts. *South Carolina Department of Archives and History.*

twenty-six or twenty-seven acres in Chick Springs Township. The nursery closed in 1945, and its charter was officially revoked in 1946.[196] Photos show the early mile markers, and some show what appears to be Paris Mountain near Greenville. Small towns and textile mills became landmarks. The double bridges (aka "twin bridges"), high bridges over the Southern and P&N Railways near Taylors, became important landmarks and reference points.

Although the Super Highway carries a U.S. number—Highway 29—it is not built as a federal highway. The U.S. numbered highway system was established in 1926 to select the best interstate highways of the day and give them a uniform numbering system to help motorists traveling around the country. One agency, the U.S. Bureau of Public Roads, helped create the numbering plan, but the roads were owned by the state highway agencies. States approved the plan by ballot of their national organization, the American Association of State Highway Officials, on November 11, 1926. The plan was strictly about highway numbering, not funds.[197]

Heavy construction machinery. *South Carolina Department of Archives and History.*

Truckers' Hill in Greer. *Photo by Scott Withrow.*

Culvert and fill over Lick Creek. *Photo by Scott Withrow.*

Twin Bridges (Taylors). *Photo by Scott Withrow.*

Not everyone knew Highway 29 as the Super Highway. In the Greer area, especially, it was sometimes known as the "Dual Lane Highway," with the name reflected in such businesses as Don's Dual Lane Shell and Dual Lane Auto Auction. In 1949, the Greenville to Greer section was dubbed Wade Hampton Boulevard, after General Wade Hampton III (1882–1902), by the Hampton Heights Women's Club.[198] A 1950 *Greenville News* article held that "Wade Hampton Boulevard" was a suggested name for a portion of the Super Highway, with no official sanction.[199] Today, the highway in the Greer and Greenville area is often referred to as Wade Hampton (Boulevard).

Highway 29, of which the Super Highway was part, began in Baltimore, Maryland's western suburbs and cut south in a western diagonal direction through the states of Virginia, North Carolina, South Carolina, Georgia and Alabama, ending at Pensacola in the Florida Panhandle. Some, because of the Florida connection, wanted it designated the Seminole Trail, but again, the designation never gained traction, at least outside Florida.[200] Although in some places, such as from Spartanburg to Greenville, it ran more east to west, it altogether ran north to south, giving it an uneven number designation, US Highway 29 (different from east–west highways, which were designated by even numbers, such as US Highway 276). Of course, if someone were traveling toward Spartanburg, it could be called the Spartanburg Highway, and toward Greenville it would be the Greenville Highway. Near its end at Stone Avenue in Greenville, a huge "million dollar" Sears Roebuck Store opened on April 7, 1949.[201] To the east of the Sears store, possibly as far as Bob Jones University and Pleasantburg Drive, the Super Highway was called by some the Great White Way because of the street lighting along that section.[202]

In 1954, granite markers were installed at every mile on the north side of the Super Highway from Greenville to North Carolina, a gift from an anonymous donor. They were installed as "a service to the motoring public," to "highway workers" and to "provide a more accurate location of accidents, buildings, or other features along the highway." They were numbered 1 through 57, with the last one at Greenville.[203] One remains from Greenville to Spartanburg.

Subsequent addition of lanes has taken away a grassy median in most places. One outstanding exception is the Super Highway as it enters Spartanburg, which has been landscaped, some of it adjacent to a residential area. This is thanks to W.O. Ezell, one of the first gardeners to take an interest in Spartanburg beautification. Conversely, the road from Greer to Greenville is, to some, visually unappealing. No section is very pedestrian friendly.

Highway 29 marker. *South Carolina Department of Archives and History.*

If the Super Highway was intended to be a "townless" parkway, it soon became busy when businesses moved out of Greer and Greenville and other municipalities to take advantage of the highway traffic. The economic future seemed to center on the Super Highway. Some businesses, such as the Super Highway Oil Company, took the name of the highway. Some of the buildings remain, but none is original. Buildings remain that once housed Culler-Jackson Furniture (Duncan area), the first Greenville Sears building, the Samoa Grill and Garrett's Texaco (Greenville). A wonderful stone house remains near St. Mark's Road in Greer, and other stone buildings remain near Taylors.

For those who drive Wade Hampton Boulevard today, it is refreshing to see photos of the road when there were few vehicles, including few large trucks. One iconic postcard shows a lone truck traveling west toward the sunset. One picture shows a young man in the grassy median with a notable cut through a ridge. Those who remember the road's early years remember few businesses and homes along the highway but instead much forestland, wheat fields and peach orchards.[204] Because of the boll weevil and other problems, cotton had become less profitable, and some upstate farmers had turned to peach growing. More peaches were grown in the upstate itself than all of Georgia.[205] Peach orchards dotted the landscape in Spartanburg and Greenville Counties, with quite a few in the Super Highway corridor, especially the Greer area, which became known for its peach-growing culture. Peach orchards—like the one near the corner of Memorial Drive and the Super Highway (now occupied by a McDonald's) and the Andrew King family orchard, near South Buncombe Road and the Super Highway (behind Staples)—are no longer there.[206]

Real estate companies first advertised homes and properties along the Super Highway, which was at the start basically rural. In 1945, one ad, for example, advertised a six-room house with hot and cold running water, a chicken house, a garage and forty peach and other fruit trees on one and a half acres near Greer.[207] The ad reflects the traditional (chicken house and orchard) but also emphasizes the new (access to the Super Highway and hot and cold water). As late as July 1, 1946, the *Greenville News* carried an ad for a "CLOSE IN FARM ON THE SUPER HIGHWAY TO SPARTANBURG, just beyond the Woodlawn Cemetery. Consists of twenty-four and ½ acres. Three springs and branches. Large enough to live on and make your living."[208] It appeared there was status to be associated with the new highway.[209] Soon, however, new subdivisions were built and advertised as being just off the Super

Postcard of the Dual Lane Highway (Super Highway). *Courtesy of Ray Belcher.*

Vanderbilt Hills subdivision. *Photo by Scott Withrow.*

Highway. Houses were advertised for their access to the Super Highway. Eventually, there were few homes left along the Super Highway, with some still remaining and repurposed for business, such as the El Matador between Greenville and Taylors. In Spartanburg, Wadsworth Hills and Vanderbilt Hills served as early housing in the area of the headwaters of Fairforest Creek near the Super Highway. Stories remain of children playing in trenches left from World War I Camp Wadsworth and of remaining camp structures.

In the Wellford community, the twenty-five-acre New Hope Farm was home to seven generations of the Snoddy family. It was significant because of its complex of domestic and agricultural buildings, listed on the National Register on May 20, 1999. Its centerpiece is the 1885 folk Victorian residence. This has changed with the construction of over two hundred one-, two- and three-bedroom apartments on the New Hope Farm property, which had its origins in 1775 and was the site of an early log home, stagecoach stop and post office.[210] Although some of the farm buildings have been removed, the iconic farmhouse remains as a café or coffee shop.[211] The New Hope acreage is only part of more than two thousand acres owned by Isaac Snoddy (1770–1842). The Scots-Irish Snoddy family became prosperous cotton farmers and members of the extended Spartanburg community.[212] James Snoddy (1954–1935), the grandson of Isaac Snoddy, owned a portable lumber mill

New Hope Victorian farmhouse. *Photo by Scott Withrow.*

and provided lumber for construction of the nearby Tucapau Mill (today's Tucapau-Startex community). Snoddy was the recipient of a shirt from some of the first cloth produced at Tucapau Mill.[213]

Driving on the early Super Highway was more of a pleasure than driving the highway today, especially at rush hour. Lore of the road abounds. One man and his wife, traveling to Spartanburg on the Super Highway, had never seen a four-lane divided highway. They were traveling east in the right lane of the left two lanes. A South Carolina highway patrolman stopped them and told the man, who was driving, that he was in the wrong lane and he needed to stay in the right lane of the right two lanes. The man did as he was told, driving all the way to Spartanburg in the right lane—but also driving back to Greer the same way! Many driving to work or otherwise remember the rhythmic sound of the expansion joints at intervals on the concrete highway. Some remember no traffic lights between Greer and Greenville.[214] Waddell family members recall stories of their grandfather crossing the Super Highway in a horse and buggy in a changing landscape of "hills, valleys, cornfields, and gullies."[215]

Despite the safety feature of a divided highway, there were accidents from the start, attributed mostly to following too closely and speeding. Drag-racing was common in some areas. In Greer, a number of senior citizens remember Highway Patrol Officer Ed Mabry, known for his tough approach to drag racers and other lawbreakers, especially bootleggers carrying moonshine from Greenville County's Dark Corner area. Moonshine runners, often in souped-up cars with powerful engines, led Mabry and other law enforcement officials on dangerous chases. Getting caught meant possible jail time but also confiscation of the moonshine and the car, which meant that officers had powerful cars.[216] The movie *Thunder Road* (1958), about a moonshine runner, negatively influenced the driving habits of many young would-be moonshine runners. Though downplayed by critics, it played to large audiences in the South, including at the Belmont Drive-In Theatre along the Super Highway in Greer and the Scenic Drive-In Theater in Spartanburg. It is now a cult classic.[217] For the first time in the movies, moonshiners were linked to cars (before, they had ridden horses). The movie showed a braking, sliding turn to avoid a roadblock. Around the South, many teens tried the moonshiner turn themselves, sometimes resulting in a roll-over.[218] Drag racing became legal with the opening of the Greer Dragway the same year (1958) as *Thunder Road*'s release. The racing site, in bottomland along Frohawk (Frohock) Creek, was less than a mile from the Super Highway.

Ed Mabry. *Courtesy of James B. McClary, South Carolina Law Officers Hall of Fame.*

It is still in operation today. Appropriately, Highway Patrol Officer Ed Mabry is buried in Wood Memorial Park at the corner of Gap Creek Road and the Super Highway.[219]

By 1939, before the completion of the Super Highway, there were thirty-one million automobiles, trucks and buses in the United States.[220] By the time of the Super Highway's completion, automobiles had become a common part of everyday life. Upstate South Carolina's Super Highway was part of a developing highway culture, known to the region and beyond. Those who grew with it, traveled to work on it and drove into the city on it have memories of restaurants or filling stations or drive-in theaters—of destinations. To some the highway is familiar, like a good friend over time. To others, it is a monster—where the destination is the goal, not the journey. The author John Steinbeck could have been writing not of New York to California but of Greenville to Spartanburg: "When we get these freeways across the whole country, as we will and must, it will be possible to drive from New York to California without seeing a single thing."[221]

Advertisement for *Thunder Road* from the *Greenville News*, September 28, 1958.

Chapter 7

BUSINESSES COME TO THE SUPER HIGHWAY

Numerous businesses have fronted on the Super Highway over the years. Chain stores now dominate, but the early Super Highway was home to local mom-and-pop businesses, many with interesting names, histories and strategies for competing. Between the Belk-Hudson store at Morgan Square and Spartanburg's Historic District west to the Super Highway Service Station at Bennett Street in Greenville, local stores and restaurants predominated. Businesses were built at various places but often near well-known landmarks such as Bob Jones University or in the small towns along the highway. They were concentrated near intersections, just as interstate businesses today locate near on and off ramps. It is important to note that the Super Highway was an interstate highway before the Interstate Highway system. Businesses served local people and travelers, and trucks served the businesses.

Among the more well-known businesses along the Spartanburg portion of the Super Highway was the Spartanburg Steeple Restaurant, a true drive-in restaurant with curb hops. Known especially for its onion rings and Dixie Burgers, it opened in 1949 and served its last meal on October 25, 2005.[222] People in Spartanburg remember the Wadsworth China Shop and its Hull Brown dip glazed pottery. Others remember the A&B Aquarium, which sold fish, fish tanks and handmade balsa fishing tackle. In Lyman, the Super Grill, advertising its air conditioning, sat near the split of the Super Highway where the National Highway composed the eastbound lanes for a time. It was just one of a number of businesses to use the words "Super" or "Dual Lane" in its business name.

Super Highway service station, from the *Greenville News*, December 15, 1938.

Culler-Jackson furniture was a landmark along the Super Highway at the Gap Creek intersection between Greer and Lyman near Duncan. Known for its American-made furniture, it advertised discount prices and payment plans in regional newspapers and on Spartanburg and Greenville television stations. An advertisement in the *Gaffney Ledger* read, "Ride a little ways and see how it pays," advertising 40 percent off.[223] It was so well known and visible that people used it as a landmark for directions. It operated for twenty-six

Culler-Jackson Furniture Store. *Courtesy of Alan Hiatt.*

years, from 1952 to the summer of 1978, and explained its closing to the public in an ad by saying that a family member had made a career change and there was no one to carry on the business. Culler-Jackson pointed out Jack Hiatt's long twenty-five-year service as manager, thanked its customers and advertised a sale.[224] Today, the building remains at the corner of Gap Creek Road and Highway 29. It is now divided into a number of businesses and is anchored by Tuck and Howell Heating, Plumbing and Air. When drivers traveling toward Greenville reach the intersection near the store, they get a good view of "Trucker's Hill," the rolling nature of the landscape and Paris Mountain beyond.

Some downtown Greer businesses began to move to locations along the Super Highway. New ones were established, again more numerous at intersections. These included drive-in theaters, restaurants, service stations, motels and oil companies. Examples included the King Cotton, Greer and Belmont drive-in theaters; the Super Highway Oil Company; and Dual Lane Auto.

The Fork, seemingly so named because it was located at the fork of West Poinsett Street and the Super Highway, was an iconic Greer restaurant, open twenty-four hours a day for many years. The owners, the Waters family, catered to both truck drivers and the general public, with truck drivers parking on the Super Highway side lot and the public on the Poinsett entrance lot. (The Super Highway was a main truck route before Interstate 85 was built.) It was known for its meat and three and especially its country-style steak. Civic groups met regularly at the Fork, and schools and other groups held banquets there. Owing to its prime site along the Super Highway, the restaurant housed an auto parts business in the back. After the restaurant closed, the auto store remained in the building.[225] Other restaurants included the Cotton Club, where Greer citizens gathered also for banquets. Iconic '60s-style restaurants abounded—Tab's Dairy Bar, the Mayfair, Horton's, Norton's and others.

Why is Culler-Jackson going out of business?

WE STARTED THIS BUSINESS IN THE EARLY FIFTIES, AND IT WAS A VERY HARD DECISION TO SHUT IT DOWN. WE HAD ONE MANAGER FOR TWENTY FIVE YEARS (MR. JACK HIATT), AND IT HAS ALWAYS BEEN A FAMILY BUSINESS. RECENTLY ONE OF THE KEY MEMBERS OF OUR FAMILY HAS DECIDED TO CHANGE CAREERS, AND THIS HAS LED TO OUR DECISION TO CLOSE OUR DOORS. WE DON'T HAVE ANYONE ELSE WHO WANTS TO MAKE A CAREER OUT OF THE BUSINESS AND THUS WE WILL SELL OR LEASE THE PROPERTY. WE HAVE APPRECIATED THE SUPPORT OF THE PEOPLE OF THE PIEDMONT OVER THE YEARS, AND WANT TO TAKE THIS OPPORTUNITY TO SAY THANKS. WE HOPE YOU WILL TAKE ADVANTAGE OF THIS SALE.

Culler-Jackson closing advertisement from the *Greenville News*, July 25, 1978.

Many businesses catered to the traveling public and truckers. These included fast-food restaurants, wrecker/towing services, garages, motels, gas stations, used and new car dealers and even an ambulance service. After all, the Super Highway was part of the main road from Charlotte to Atlanta, and there were wrecks and breakdowns from the beginning. Travelers sought food and restrooms.

The intersection on the Super Highway called Appalache Crossing has seen businesses thrive and wane. Appalache Road led to the Appalache Mill community, while Arlington Road south led to downtown Greer. In the early years of the highway, this intersection was a hot spot for business. Don's Dual Lane Shell Service Station at the Appalache Crossing combined many of these services to gain business from both area persons and travelers. In addition to operating a service station, Don Edwards sold used cars and cigarettes at price (to bring in customers to sell more gas), owned an auto auction and provided a wrecker and ambulance service. Paul Green remembers that young people "hung out" inside playing pinball.[226] Edwards, it can be said, "had cornered the market"—at least the corner at Appalache Crossing.

Gas stations were often creative. At one ESSO station, those who filled up with high test received a Dragnet badge and at times a tiger

Top: The Fork Restaurant interior. *Courtesy of Tony Waters.*

Bottom: The Fork Restaurant, from a *Greer Citizen* ad, April 16, 1953.

tail. Some people would hang one from their gas tank caps. They were following the ESSO advertising theme, "Put a Tiger in Your Tank—with ESSO."[227] Esso tiger art was featured in vintage posters until Esso rebranded itself as Exxon in 1973 with a new logo. But the tiger left a legacy with collectors and those who remember a bygone era of service with a smile, a time when service station operators would wash a car's windows and check the oil.[228]

Automobile dealer Jim Benson is emblematic of the work ethic among Super Highway entrepreneurs. His Memory Lane Museum reflects the car culture of the Super Highway and is a tribute to the 1950s. The grandson of a Travelers Rest sharecropper, he started with $200. Beginning with a paper route, he moved on to hauling and selling used cars, finally establishing a profitable Chrysler auto dealership when Ford and General Motors vehicles were popular in the area. To many, Benson epitomizes the American dream—finding a career you like, sticking to it and thriving.[229]

The early years of the Super Highway saw the era of motor courts and motels when people were perhaps first exposed to wall-to-wall carpets, sliding-glass doors, vinyl upholstery and air conditioning. It was home

Jim Benson Memory Lane Museum. *Photo by Scott Withrow.*

decorating unlike anything people had seen.[230] Although some motels along the entire Super Highway route have been refurbished or repurposed, many now exist only as images on postcards.

In Greer, the Holiday Motel, across the road from the King Cotton Drive-In Theater, offered one of three public swimming pools in the area. Just down the Super Highway was Suttle's Puddle, the pool owned by the Suttle family. Just out of Greer, in the Taylors area, was the swimming lake at Chick Springs. The building of the Super Highway and its later expansion reduced the size of the lake.

Skyline Motor Court, on a hillside eight miles from Greenville along the Super Highway and just outside Greer, is an example of a repurposed hotel for a time, perhaps not to everyone's liking. The original motel was AAA-rated, and it also displayed the seal of Quality Courts, an informal group of operators that set motel standards. Even more prestigious was the Duncan Hines recommendation found in the 1954 edition of Hines's *Lodging for a Night*. The entry listed the Skyline Motor Court along the Dual Lane and stated that it had ten rooms, modern furniture, combination tub and shower tile baths and York heating and air conditioning. Rooms were four dollars, six dollars and up.[231] Hines was a traveling salesman who often ate in restaurants and lodged in many hotels/motels, some of which he recommended. His recommendations were turned into annual books on lodging and eating. His recommendation of the Skyline Motor Court meant that he had lodged there.[232] The hotel was later repurposed into a lounge, which over time had various names, including Toby's, LB's, Billy Bobs and Under the Moon. It was torn down a number of years ago.

The Buttonwood Motor Court stood alongside the Super Highway's juncture with St. Mark's Road. Postcard photos show a neat-looking, well-landscaped motel of the early motor court type. The parking area appears to be lightly graveled or cemented and bordered by rocks, painted white to designate parking spots. The office was taller, perhaps two stories, with wings and rooms attached to either side. Early motor courts debated over whether to have parking garages adjacent to the rooms, but for most, that meant fewer rooms and therefore less income. Guests in those days enjoyed the convenience of unloading directly in front of their rooms.[233]

Bypassed by Interstate 85 in the early 1960s, many of these motels struggled—some are still struggling—to stay afloat, and some, like the Holiday, Skyline and Buttonwood, were torn down. The Super Highway

Skyline Motor Court. *Richard Sawyer Collection.*

changed with the times, and today there are few iconic motels or restaurants to be found, as is the case along segments of other historic highways such as Route 66.

Taverns with colorful names such as the Rusty Nail, the Tic Toc and Sarge's were also located along the highway, some well known to law enforcement in the area. One story is that of a minister of a local church who passed the collection plate and received few offerings. He threatened to go to a nearby tavern on Saturday night and record license plates in the parking lot. He again passed the plate at church and garnered a substantial offering.[234] The Sand Trap at the corner of Reid School Road was a long-standing tavern site, catering to those who wanted to practice their putting game out back.

The El Matador Mexican Restaurant is perhaps the oldest business and the oldest building along the Super Highway. The one-hundred-seat restaurant is in an inconspicuous stone house between Taylors and Greenville. When it opened in 1968, Mexican food was new to many in the upstate. It does not advertise and doesn't have gleaming polished metal walls; yet, it has devoted customers, often multigenerational. Ownership, too, is generational, since the restaurant has been owned by the same family since its inception. Moreover, according to some, it has the distinction of being the oldest Mexican restaurant in South Carolina.[235]

The El Matador restaurant. *Photo by Scott Withrow.*

Before it was a restaurant, it was a family home. Those whose family members lived in the house remember a well for water, woods in the back, figs or other fruit trees, a separate stone garage (still there) and a magnolia tree in the front yard. Part of the house was rented as an apartment. There was a deep drainage ditch in the front where kids played and watched the traffic on the Super Highway. It was quite a house, likely built in the early days of the Super Highway by an unknown, highly skilled stonemason, who likely built other stone houses in the area. Putting names to the home—the Sorbet family lived there—gives even more meaning to this historic home.[236]

The stone house at the corner of St. Mark's Road and the Super Highway, built by 1950, still remains at this writing. Home at one time to Corra Lee McCarter Steadman Monk and family, it was adjacent to Bull family property and across the road and up the hill from the Chick Springs Resort property. Camellias still bloom and shade-loving plans still thrive, some of which are the work of Mrs. Steadman (Monk upon her first husband's death and her remarriage), who, according to family members, had a green thumb. It was in some ways a country house with a well and a rectangular in-ground storage area (perhaps a root cellar) for fruits or vegetables.[237] No records have been found of the stonemason who built this and other stone houses in the area.

Early stone house on the Super Highway in Greer. *Photo by Scott Withrow.*

Drive-in theaters, popular in the '40s and '50s, were especially popular along the Super Highway. There were four: the Greer Drive-In, owned by H.P. McManus; the Belmont, near the double bridges—aka Twin Bridges—at Taylors; the King Cotton, across from the Holiday Motel in Greer; and the Highway 29 Drive-In in Clevedale in Spartanburg. At one point, Nick Belmont of Spartanburg owned three drive-ins: one in Spartanburg, the King Cotton at Greer and the Belmont near Taylors. The King Cotton advertised its opening with the movie *The Stratton Story* about a baseball pitcher from Texas. The theater advertised itself as one of the most modern drive-in theaters in the South.

At one point and into the 1990s, Dawson Dill operated a popular miniature (putt-putt) and par-three golf course. Dill Creek, a tributary of the Enoree, flowed through the property. It is now the site of Dill Creek Commons Shopping Center, of which the late Mr. Dill was part owner.[238]

Allen Bennett Memorial Hospital served the Greer community along the Super Highway for over fifty years (1952–2008) until Greer Memorial Hospital was completed at a new site. (The Allen Bennett building was later torn down, and the Jim Benson auto dealership expanded to that site.)

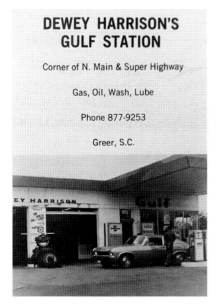

DEWEY HARRISON'S GULF STATION

Corner of N. Main & Super Highway

Gas, Oil, Wash, Lube

Phone 877-9253

Greer, S.C.

Left: Dewey Harrison's Gulf station. *Greer Heritage Museum.*

Below: Wingo's Motel and Esso Service Station. *Courtesy of Tony Waters.*

WINGO'S MOTEL & SERVICE STATION
Highway 29–20 Miles South of Spartanburg, S. C.

William W. Burgiss, cotton mill magnate and millionaire philanthropist, envisioned either a hospital or technical college on the site of his peach orchard at a place he named Air Castle Heights. This never occurred after a 1949 court decision allowed the development of Burgiss Hills, Greer's "premier upscale residential community."[239] Instead, Burgiss founded W.W. Burgiss Charities and funded such noteworthy projects as the first Greenville Shriners Children's Hospital. His charitable organization still exists.[240]

The Super Highway at rush hour. *Photo by Scott Withrow.*

The Super Highway has been home to many businesses. It is impossible to mention all of them. Some, such as Dewey Harrison's Gulf Service Station in Greer, were landmarks. Some moved from the Greer area to do business alongside the highway at some point. Bond's Furniture was one of those, thriving for years alongside the Super Highway. Dobson's Hardware, a longtime Greer business, still survives alongside the highway as a repurposed business, Dobson Gifts and General Hardware. The El Matador remains beyond Taylors, and the Clock near Bob Jones University is a fixture at the corner of Pleasantburg Road and the Super Highway. These and other businesses have been part of the history of one of the best-known boulevards in upstate South Carolina.

The Taylors to Greenville section of the Super Highway saw the creation of a number of businesses and institutions during its boom years in the 1940s and '50s. It included the following.

BOB JONES UNIVERSITY

Bob Jones College relocated to Greenville during the boom years of the 1940s and the first years of the Super Highway. It was founded by its namesake, Bob Jones Sr., in 1927 in Bay County, Florida. Subsequently, the college moved to Cleveland, Tennessee, in 1933. Having no further space to expand, the college set its sights on moving to Knoxville, Tennessee, until certain people in Greenville, familiar with the college, lured it to the town. Among those working to get Bob Jones College to establish a campus in Greenville were real estate agent E. Roy Stone and members of the Greenville Chamber of Commerce. Bob Jones College began construction of a new campus in 1946 in Greenville along the newly completed Super Highway on land described as full of "hills, valleys, cornfields, and gullies." The chamber subsequently provided $96,000 of the original $175,000 asking price for 180 acres of land. One of the chamber's first acts was to erect a large billboard along the Super Highway with the words, "Future Home of Bob Jones University, Beginning Fall of 1947."[241] Construction executive Charles E. Daniel was selected to construct the campus within another school year in a $3 million building program.[242]

With the land still muddy from construction, the institution officially became Bob Jones University at its dedication on Thanksgiving Day 1947. (The school used the university designation on its stationery before its move from Tennessee.)[243] Although it had a rocky relationship with the City of Greenville, Bob Jones University spurred economic growth along the Super Highway. The university's "ultramodern campus" of light yellow brick reflected Charles Daniel's influence and that of Greenville's industrial base.[244] Over the years, Bob Jones became known for its fine arts program and its internationally recognized collection of Baroque art.[245] Faculty such as the late Carl Blair (1932–2018) exemplified Bob Jones's commitment to the visual arts. (See chapter 8, "Buried at Cemeteries Along the Super Highway.")

Bob Jones University continues as a Christian liberal arts institution and has branched into publishing for the homeschool curriculum.

CAROLE'S RECORD SHOP

Carole's Record Shop was a thriving business for many years along Wade Hampton Boulevard. Starting first at Wade Hampton Mall in 1962, it had moved by 1973 to a new building nearby. Over the years, it was known as Carole's Record Shop and Boutique and Carole's Record and Hi-Fi Shop. The new, uniquely designed building with a center portion that looked similar to a turntable later housed a camera shop and still stands along Wade Hampton Boulevard.[246]

DIXIE–HOME STORES WAREHOUSE (WINN-DIXIE)

In 1948, the Dixie–Home Stores of Greenville began construction of a large grocery warehouse on the Super Highway four and a half miles out of Greenville. The warehouse was built as a central distribution center for the 150-plus stores owned by Dixie–Home Stores in North Carolina, South Carolina and Georgia. Out of that number, 83 were supermarkets. The Furman University Foundation leased the warehouse for twenty-five years with the option to renew the contract. The warehouse was built by the Daniel Construction Company of Greenville with the Sloan Company of Greenville as the subcontractor. It was designed by the McPherson Company and was completed in 1949 at a cost of approximately $1,500,000.[247]

The large warehouse was 968 feet long and 240 feet wide and was the largest of its kind in the Southeast at the time. It was built on the former Edwards property near the mainline of the Southern Railway, which ran from New Orleans to Washington, D.C. A long double siding track was built from the mainline to service the warehouse. The main section of the warehouse covered more than 200,000 square feet and the office area covered 18,000 square feet. The Dixie–Home Stores warehouse had individual sections for the meat department, produce department, grocery department and maintenance shop. The meat and produce departments had areas for cold storage and refrigeration. The company owned its own fleet of trucks. When the warehouse opened in 1949, it was one of the most modern and highly mechanized facilities of its kind in the United States.[248]

An open house was held in November 1949 to allow members of the community to tour the new facility. During an eleven-hour span, an estimated

Above: Carole's Record Shop. *Courtesy of Carole Greene-Henderson.*

Left: Carole's Record Shop interior. *Courtesy of Carole Greene-Henderson.*

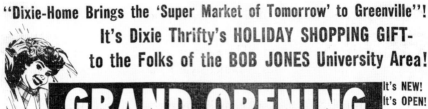

Winn-Dixie advertisement from the *Greenville News*, December 15, 1938.

fifteen thousand visitors took thirty-minute guided tours of the warehouse. State Highway Patrol officers handled the traffic flow, and parking was available for three thousand vehicles. At the end of each thirty-minute tour, visitors were provided with a buffet-style meal that included ham, beef, turkey, bread, salad and punch.[249]

Dixie–Home Stores of Greenville merged with the Winn & Lovett Grocery Company of Florida in 1955 and became Winn-Dixie Stores. As a result of this merger, Winn-Dixie Stores became the most profitable grocery chain in the United States from the mid-1950s to the mid-1960s.[250] In 1987, the merged company paid $6.5 million for the warehouse and surrounding land.[251] The Winn-Dixie warehouse closed its doors in 2005.[252]

GREENVILLE STEEL AND FOUNDRY

The Greenville Steel and Foundry Company was founded in 1924. It began as a small foundry and shop on Markley Street in Greenville. In 1940, the company moved to a more spacious location near the intersection of the Super Highway and the old Camp Road that ran through Camp Sevier during World War I.

A brick building, built in 1940, served as the office along with space for the drafting and engineering departments. The foundry section was in a large building that resembled an airplane hangar. Southern Railway and Piedmont and Northern Railway added siding tracks for the shipping and receiving of materials. During World War II, the company manufactured parts for the building of LSTs (Landing Ship, Tank), LSMs (Landing Ship Medium), destroyer-escorts and barges, in addition to parts for textile machinery.

The company made small brass plates that were shipped to Tennessee for the program developing the atomic bomb. Everything from blueprints to scrap material used had to be packed and returned since the U.S. Espionage Act covered the entire process of what was a top-secret project related to the World War II era. The company produced material for the building of army installations such as the Greenville Army Air Base and Camp Croft (Spartanburg) and also manufactured parts that were used in the building of ships at the naval yard in Charleston. Bulkheads were made for LSMs, which were amphibious assault ships. The company made the bulkhead for LSM-139, which was shown in the famous photograph of General Douglas MacArthur wading ashore at Leyte in the Pacific in 1945. In addition, Greenville Steel made parts for army transportation barges that were towed by other vessels and carried items such as oil and food. The company also manufactured parts for vessels used by Great Britain. Foundations for twenty-millimeter guns on destroyer-escorts were also fabricated in Greenville. The work done by Greenville Steel and Foundry was an important part of South Carolina's contribution to the war effort during World War II.[253]

PET DAIRY PRODUCTS COMPANY

The Pet Dairy Products Company opened in a three-story building at the Super Highway entrance in Greenville in January 1947. But it was not new to Greenville, having begun operations on February 1, 1944. Pet established its business in Greenville after buying dairies that included Sanitary Dairies and Chapman's Dairy. By 1958, it employed more than two hundred people and had about ninety delivery trucks.[254]

Local dairy farmers in the upstate provided fresh milk to Pet Dairy, where it was processed. Joseph Johnson of Travelers Rest was one among other dairy farmers. In 1958, he had forty milk cows, which he fed a special mixed formula of oats, cottonseed and corn with molasses. He kept the milk cooled at about thirty-five degrees before placing it in ten-gallon cans for transportation to Pet Dairy. Johnson's dairy produced over four thousand pounds of milk each week.[255]

THE BELMONT DRIVE-IN THEATRE

The first drive-in movie theater in the United States opened in New Jersey in 1933. Richard Hollingshead came up with the idea, history records, because his mother had talked about how uncomfortable movie theater seats were. Hollingshead experimented in his own driveway before opening what he called a "Park-In Theater."

In August 1949, the Belmont Drive-In Theatre opened on the dual-lane Super Highway with parking spaces for five hundred vehicles at a cost of

$100,000 to construct. The parking area was tiered so that moviegoers could have a better view of the large wooden framed screen.[256] It had some of its own characteristics, but in many ways, it was like many others in the United States.

The parking surface was paved with tar and gravel by the Willimon Grading Company of Greenville.[257] The drive-in was located approximately three miles north of Bob Jones University near the Super Highway's dual bridges that crossed over both the Southern Railway and Piedmont and Northern Railway lines.[258]

The projectors and in-car speakers with individual volume control were installed by the Theatre Equipment Company of Charlotte, North Carolina. The plumbing for the Belmont was installed by the Taylors Plumbing Company of Greer. The fixtures for the concession stand were installed by the Satterfield Woodwork Shop of Greer.[259]

The Belmont Drive-In Theatre opened on August 29, 1949, with the largest screen in South Carolina at the time.[260] Admission was forty cents for adults. Children under twelve were admitted for free. A playground and rides on a fire truck were provided for children.[261] The feature that was shown on opening night was *Abbott & Costello Meet Frankenstein*.[262] After twenty-nine years of operation, the Belmont Drive-In Theatre was closed and demolished in 1978.

Nicholas "Nick" Estatious Belmont, the theater's owner and general manager, was a native of Greece who came to America in 1902. He settled first in Spartanburg and lived there for seventeen years, where he was superintendent of the dye department at Reeves Brothers. He married Maybell McArthur and later lived in Taylors for thirteen years. He and his family were members of the Episcopal Church of the Good Shepherd, in Greer. He lived along Watson Road in Taylors, about a half mile from the Belmont Drive-In. He died on Christmas Day 1967, and he and other family members are buried at Wood Memorial Park, in the Duncan area, just off the Super Highway.[263]

Belmont Drive-In Theatre ad from the *Greenville News* August 28, 1949.

Above: Henry's Smokehouse. *Photo by Mike Boone.*

Below: Sunset Inn, Greenville. *Photo by Mike Boone.*

UNIVERSITY SINCLAIR SERVICE STATION

In the 1950s, the University Sinclair Service Station stood along the Super Highway.[264] It was next to Bob Jones University and across the highway from Woodlawn Memorial Park Cemetery. John Herman Affalter, the owner, was a saddle horse trainer who moved from Kansas to Greenville.[265]

The station was known for its many promotions. One involved the burning of a large candle, and customers were asked to guess how long the candle would burn. The winner of the contest received a set of white sidewall tires.[266] Affalter made use of his horse-training skills, offering free horseback riding lessons with the purchase of ten gallons of gas or an oil change.[267] Another giveaway was a Quarter Horse that was won by a Bob Jones University graduate. In another promotion, the owner gave away free stamp collections and comic books. The Sinclair Company developed a product called RD-119, which received a United States patent. RD-119 was a chemical added to gasoline to inhibit rust. Sinclair even published a comic book about the development and use of RD-119 that Affalter and other Sinclair owners gave to customers.[268]

Affalter was a great promoter, creating such ads as "What you do is your business. Our business is to serve you and promptly." His talents extended beyond his promotions; he was also a good golfer, recording a hole in one on the seventh hole of the Hillandale Golf Course in Greenville using a five-iron.[269]

For those of you wondering how long the large candle burned, it burned for 135 hours and 12 minutes.[270]

Chapter 8

BURIED AT CEMETERIES ALONG THE SUPER HIGHWAY

WOODLAWN MEMORIAL PARK

If you travel the route of what was the Super Highway from Greenville to Spartanburg today, you will pass the Woodlawn Memorial Park about a mile and a half east of Greenville and beyond Bob Jones University. At its opening in 1939, headlines in the local newspaper emphasized its location on the "super-boulevard." An advertisement referred to it as a "garden of memories to serve Greenville's greater needs."

Before work began on Woodlawn Memorial Park, a survey was made of the other burial facilities in Greenville. Woodlawn was developed as a non-monumental, garden-type cemetery, the first of its kind in the area. The design called for a system of paved driveways throughout the park and included a beautiful double drive entrance on the Super Highway. Its layout included a Tower of Chimes, parklike lawns and lakes, the latter never built. The chosen site was a sixty-one-acre tract of land, of which two-thirds was still under development when it opened in 1939 at a cost of approximately $100,000 for the first phase of development. The entrance on the Super Highway included portals made from Balfour granite, a pink to cream-colored granite quarried near Balfour in Henderson County, North Carolina.

The first superintendent of Woodlawn Memorial Park was George Hyatt, who came to Greenville with thirty years of experience managing a

Woodlawn Memorial Park. *Photo by Scott Withrow.*

cemetery in Toledo, Ohio. He and his family moved into a residence on the grounds of the memorial park, while a sales office for the disposal of plots was established at the Woodside Building in Greenville. Offices were moved from downtown Greenville to Woodlawn on January 22, 1939. Officers of Woodlawn Memorial Park in 1939 were President C.M. Gaffney, Vice President E.M. Blythe Sr. and Secretary Treasurer L.L. McGirt Jr. Directors included Colonel E.M. Blythe (Blythe and Bonham, attorneys, Greenville), Joseph H. Britt (Britt-McKinney Company, food brokers, Greenville), Clyde M. Gaffney (realtor, Greenville), Frank S. Smith (McAlister, Smith, and Pate, investments, Greenville), William Wallace (Palmetto State Life Insurance Company, Columbia) and J.P. Williamson (Dixie–Home Stores, Greenville).

Work on Woodlawn Memorial Park began in October 1939 with a crew that ranged from fifteen to thirty-five men. The plans from the beginning called for a permanent staff to care for the grounds, the tower and the burial plots and to allow the park to always have the appearance of a landscaped garden. Free transportation was provided in 1939 for anyone wishing to visit the cemetery.

Woodlawn Memorial Park was designed to be a cemetery without tombstones of varying shapes and sizes. At the time of its opening, it was the only non-monumental burial estate in Greenville. The architect of Woodlawn Memorial Park was Hugh R. Chapman. Williams Hardware Company in Travelers Rest, which sold cement, lumber and builder supplies, furnished some of the materials for the development of the cemetery.[271]

Major Rudolf Anderson, U.S. Air Force

Major Rudolf Anderson, an American Air Force pilot, was the only U.S. fatality during the Cuban Missile Crisis of October 1962. Major Anderson was shot down and killed while flying his U-2F Dragon Lady aircraft over Cuba on a reconnaissance mission over the island country. Major Anderson was a native South Carolinian who was born in Spartanburg and grew up in Greenville, where he attended Augusta Circle Elementary School and graduated from Greenville High School in 1944. A former classmate of his at Augusta Circle Elementary School once said that Anderson was always drawing airplanes in class. As a member of Boy Scout Troop 19 under Scoutmaster Roy Gullick, a veteran of World War II, Anderson earned the rank of Eagle Scout. In 1948, he graduated from Clemson University, where he was a member of the Air Force Reserve Officers Training Corps. Upon

RUDOLF ANDERSON, JR

MAJOR U.S. AIR FORCE

SEPTEMBER 15   OCTOBER 27
1927   1962

SON OF
RUDOLF AND MARY ANDERSON

KOREA

CUBAN MISSILE CRISIS
AIR FORCE CROSS

Left: Major Rudolf Anderson. *The National Museum of the United States Air Force.*

Right: Major Rudolf Anderson Memorial. *Photo by Scott Withrow.*

graduation, he was commissioned as a second lieutenant in the United States Air Force. He began his career in the Air Force as an F-86 Sabre pilot and served with distinction during the Korean War.[272]

Major Anderson was laid to rest on November 6, 1962, in Woodlawn Memorial Park, where approximately 1,800 people were gathered for his service. Those in attendance included General Thomas S. Power, commander in chief of the U.S. Strategic Air Command (SAC). Major Anderson was buried with full military honors and awarded the Distinguished Service Medal posthumously. He was also the first recipient of the Air Force Cross, the second-highest award and decoration for valor of the U.S. military and Air Force. The Elite Guard of the Strategic Air Command was present at the graveside service. As the flag-draped coffin was carried to the grave site, a flight of U.S. Air Force jets flew over Woodlawn Memorial Park with the no. 2 position in the formation missing in a salute to Major Anderson. At the end of the graveside service, the flag was lowered by the color guard while a volley of rifle shots was fired in a salute. After a bugler played "Taps," the chimes sounded in the cemetery's Tower of Chimes to end the service.[273]

A memorial to Major Anderson stands today at Cleveland Park in Greenville. An F-86 Sabre jet like the type that Anderson flew in the Korean War is a part of the memorial, which was officially dedicated in May 1963.

There is also a permanent exhibit about Major Anderson at the Major Rudolf Anderson Jr. American Legion Post 214 and Cecil D. Buchanan Military History Museum located on Wade Hampton Boulevard (former Super Highway) in Greenville.

Klaus Martin Einstein

Most people know that Albert Einstein was born in Germany in the late 1800s and became one of the most famous scientists in the world by the time of his death in 1955. Many people may not know about Einstein's connection to Greenville, South Carolina. In 1938, Albert Einstein's son, Hans Einstein, came to Greenville with his family from Switzerland to work for the Soil Conservation Service of the United States Department of Agriculture. Hans Einstein was an engineer who specialized in the research of sediment transport. He worked on a project on the Enoree River during his time in Greenville.[274] In 1934, Spartanburg had been selected as the headquarters of the Southeastern Division of the Soil Conservation Service to work with local farmers in the area. Methods for soil erosion control and soil reclamation were developed. The Southeastern Division worked on such things as crop diversification, care of wildlife, the development of grazing

Klaus Martin Einstein Memorial. *Photo by Scott Withrow.*

for dairying and the management of forest products.[275] While Hans was living in Greenville, his son Klaus Martin passed away in January 1939 at the age of five. Klaus died of complications related to diphtheria. He is buried in Woodlawn Memorial Park. In May 1941, Albert Einstein came to Greenville to visit his son Hans and took time to visit the campus of Furman University, which was in downtown Greenville at the time.[276]

"Shoeless" Joe Jackson

Joseph Jefferson Jackson, better known as "Shoeless Joe," was born in Pickens County, South Carolina, in 1887. His family moved to Greenville to work at Brandon Mill, a textile mill on the west side of Greenville. By the time he was eight years old, Joe Jackson was working in the mill. Textile League baseball was very popular in the region in the first half of the twentieth century. Jackson began playing on the Brandon Mill baseball team when he was thirteen years old. He soon made a name for himself as an outfielder and hitter of home runs. In 1908, Jackson played minor-league baseball for the

Joe Jackson with the Brandon Mill team. *Courtesy of Jim Wilson.*

Joe Jackson Memorial. *Photo by Scott Withrow.*

Greenville Spinners. During that season, he played a game in his stocking feet because his new shoes were uncomfortable. A local newspaper writer tagged him with the nickname "Shoeless Joe," and the nickname stuck with him for the rest of his life. Jackson began his Major League Baseball career in 1908. During his career, he played for the Philadelphia Athletics, Cleveland Naps and Chicago White Sox. "Shoeless Joe" Jackson was one of eight White Sox players banned from baseball for life in 1920. The commissioner of baseball banned them for what became known as the "Black Sox Scandal" for the throwing of the 1919 World Series. Joe Jackson's career batting average was .356, the third highest in Major League Baseball history. After his baseball career ended, Jackson came back to Greenville to live. "Shoeless Joe" passed away in Greenville in 1951 and is buried at Woodlawn Memorial Park. The Shoeless Joe Jackson Museum and Baseball Library is in Greenville and is open to the public.[277]

Frank Hamblen

Francis Griscom "Frank" Hamblen, a native of Humansville, Missouri, moved to Greenville in 1920. He was living in Rogers, Arkansas, at the time and came to Greenville as a railroad executive. He was the vice president and general manager of the Greenville and Northern (G&N) Railroad from 1920 until his retirement in 1957. Hamblen was also the vice president and general manager of the Saluda Land and Lumber Company. The G&N ran from Greenville to River Falls in northern Greenville County. The railroad ran steam locomotives from the 1920s to the 1940s before switching to diesel locomotives. The train was known as the "Swamp Rabbit." The former rail line of the G&N Railroad is now part of the Swamp Rabbit Trail, which is a popular hiking and biking trail. In Greenville, Frank Hamblen was an active civic leader. He served as president of the Greenville Chamber of Commerce and chairman of the Greenville Civil Service Commission. Hamblen was awarded the Silver Beaver by the Blue Ridge Council of the Boy Scouts of America in 1940 for his work and support of Scouting. On a national level, Hamblen served on the board of the American Short Line Railroad Association and on a committee of the Interstate Commerce Commission. Frank Hamblen died in 1958 and is interred at Woodlawn Memorial Park.[278]

Dick Dietz

Dick Dietz was born in Crawfordsville, Indiana, in 1941. He was a Greenville High School graduate. After finishing high school, Dietz signed a Major League Baseball contract.[279] Dietz played in the National League with the San Francisco Giants from 1966 to 1971, the Los Angeles Dodgers in 1972 and the Atlanta Braves in 1973. After retiring as a major-league player, he served as a minor-league coach and manager for three different teams from 1993 to 1999. Dietz was a catcher for most of his major-league career. He was a National League All-Star in 1970. Dick Dietz played in 646 major-league games and finished with a .261 career batting average. Dick Dietz passed away in 2005. He is buried at Woodlawn Memorial Park.[280]

Carl Blair

A native of Kansas, Carl Blair (November 28, 1932–January 22, 2018) was an artist and art teacher who joined the faculty of Bob Jones University in 1957 and taught there for forty years.[281] His daughter, Ruth Blair Lair, remembers that he also taught nights at the Greenville County Museum of Art for twenty years. He received numerous awards over the years. He was awarded the Order of the Palmetto by the South Carolina governor on January 22, 2018. He also received the 2005 Elizabeth O'Neill Verner Governor's Award for the Arts for Lifetime Achievement in the Arts.[282]

Carl Blair and his daughter, Ruth Blair Lair. *Courtesy of Ruth Blair Lair.*

In 2013, Greenville's Metropolitan Arts Council created the Carl R. Blair Award "for commitment to art education." He influenced many artists, and the council subsequently recognized forty-five artists who had been influenced by him.[283] Blair was described as a "master teacher," "superb artist" and a "driving force in the South Carolina arts scene" who influenced numerous artists over generations.[284]

For his own art, he was known for his colorful landscapes, influenced by his youth on a Kansas farm. Many of these came from his intuitive imagination.[285] This was all the more amazing because he was colorblind; he could only detect cool colors (blues and greens) versus warm colors (reds and oranges).[286]

He and his wife had little money in their early years in Greenville, "not having two nickels to rub together," as described by their only daughter, Ruth. They lived in faculty housing, and Carl worked a second job. Eventually, they built their dream home in a Frank Lloyd Wright style on nearby Paris Mountain. The architect, Jim Neal, was a friend of Carl's and accepted paintings in lieu of money for his architectural design. On Paris Mountain, the Blairs were surrounded by the "land, woods, and animals," which inspired Carl's paintings.[287]

Carl and his wife, Margaret Elaine Ruble Blair, are buried at Woodlawn Memorial Park.[288]

Eve Robertson

There are famous and near famous who are buried along the Super Highway, but there are also people, seemingly obscure, who made a name for themselves far beyond the Greenville area, even internationally. One person especially fits this description—Eve (Eva) Robertson.

Eva Tate Robertson grew up in the Sandy Flat community west of Greer, but she is identified most with her home on a wooded hill in a subdivision just off the Super Highway in the larger Taylors community. Here, she and her husband, Ben, the Taylors postmaster, lived in a modest home. She is remembered by many for her love of daffodils, for growing them, hybridizing them and developing numerous new varieties. The couple so identified with daffodils that they named their home and property Daffodale.[289]

Eve Robertson had been fascinated with daffodils since the age of six. Her interest in hybridizing daffodils received a boost when she began corresponding with Guy Wilson, a hybridizer in Northern Ireland. She wrote to him for many years and received replies. He died before she got to meet him, but on a tour of England, Scotland and Ireland, she met Wilson's widow and leading hybridizers in Ireland. One of the highlights of the trip was attending the London Daffodil Show, perhaps the world's finest showing of daffodils.[290]

Eve Robertson was one of only three upstate daffodil hybridizers in 1963 (the others being Dan Thompson of Clemson and William Gould Jr., then of Greer).[291] At the time of a 1963 newspaper article on her work, she had been hybridizing daffodils for twenty years. During this time and into her nineties, she spoke to many garden clubs locally and across the country and often spoke of the patience required in hybridizing—of cross-pollinating and waiting four or five years for a plant to produce flowers and for the bulbs to multiply. Amazingly, she developed sixteen new varieties, including the Gladys Meadors, the Agnes Ivy, the Yellow Glow and the Promenade.[292]

Eve Robertson daffodils. *Courtesy of Frances Worthington.*

Frances Worthington, a garden writer for many years for the *Greenville News*, was one of the last to interview Robertson and wrote of her patience in the process of cross-pollinating.[293] Worthington wrote about Robertson's

Eve Robertson. *Courtesy of Frances Worthington.*

membership in the American Daffodil Society and noted that she was asked by that organization to be a judge in daffodil shows, She went on to judge many shows, including a show in London, and to train judges. Worthington wrote of additional hybrids Robertson developed—Elegant Lady, Limey Circle and Angel Silk.[294]

Beyond the science of hybridizing, there were many who remember Eve Robertson and her positive personality, along with her friends "from London to Oregon."[295] An article on her passing in the March 2003 edition of the *Daffodil Journal* speaks of these friendships:

> *Mary Price and I were able to visit with Eve at length in her home, "Daff-o-Dale," sitting up late at night talking over her "stud book," and by day walking through her large "daffodil patch," where she knew the name and provenance of every cultivar and seedling. Linda Wallpe said it well: "Eve was a lesson in how to attack life with grace and good humor," even through loss and many illnesses and increasing infirmity. She was the youngest 96-year-old one could imagine. I never heard her talk about "the good old days." For Eve, today was the second best day of all time; the best day would be some morning next spring when her daffodils would first open, or she would go to convention and see her host of friends.[296]*

One friend summed it best: "She was a gracious lady, a superb grower of daffodils, a successful hybridizer, and a good friend to all who shared her interest in daffodils."[297]

Eve Robertson died on February 2, 2003, at the age of ninety-six.[298] She was an internationally known daffodil expert living a quarter of a mile or so off the Super Highway and whose final resting place is Woodlawn, along the Super Highway.

HILLCREST MEMORIAL GARDENS

Hillcrest Memorial Gardens, located at the crest of what was known as Truckers' Hill along the Super Highway, is a modern memorial park cemetery.

Carl Story

Carl Story was a pioneer in developing a type of music known as bluegrass gospel.[299] Story grew up in western North Carolina, where he learned to play the fiddle at the age of nine. In 1934, he organized his first band, known as the Rambling Mountaineers, in reply to the question from band members: "Carl, what are you going to name us?" His answer: "If we play to make any money at this, we'll be doing a lot of rambling, and we're all from the North Carolina mountains; so we will call our band the Rambling Mountaineers."[300] From 1935 until 1942, Story was a member of the Lonesome Mountaineers. In 1942, Story began a short stint with Bill Monroe, known as the "Father of Bluegrass," and his Blue Grass Boys. Carl Story was drafted in 1943 and served in the United States Navy until the end of World War II in 1945.[301]

Carl Story. *Courtesy of Caldwell Heritage Museum, Lenoir, North Carolina.*

From the late 1940s until he passed away in 1995, Carl Story recorded with different record labels and worked at different radio stations, including WCKI in Greer.[302] During the 1970s, 1980s and early 1990s, Story performed at bluegrass festivals around the country.[303] Randy "Country" Hawkins of Travelers Rest, South Carolina, remembers seeing Story perform in the 1980s at Hendersonville High School (in North Carolina) on a Saturday night and then again at Blue Ridge High School (in South Carolina) the following weekend.[304]

In retirement, Story lived in Greer and worked as a disc jockey until he passed away in 1995.[305] He is buried at Hillcrest Memorial Gardens in Greer.

WOOD MEMORIAL PARK

Wood Memorial Park was established in 1952 as a memorial park cemetery with markers at lawn level. It is located along Gap Creek Road, its entrance within sight of the Super Highway. Burials include people from the Lyman-

Duncan-Greer area. Among well-known persons buried there are baseball player Flint Rhem and well-known local highway patrolman Ed Mabry.

Charles Flint Rhem

Charles Flint Rhem, professional baseball player, was born on January 24, 1901, in Williamsburg County in South Carolina's Lowcountry near coastal Georgetown. His father, Furnifold Rhem, was in the cotton, naval stores and steamship business. Rhem, in fact, named his son after the New York shipbuilder Charles Flint, a friend and business associate. Flint Rhem, however, did not remain in Lowcountry South Carolina; he gained fame as a professional baseball player.

Over his career, he was a pitcher for the St. Louis Cardinals, Philadelphia Phillies and Boston Braves and pitched against such players as Babe Ruth, who hit two home runs off him in the 1926 World Series. Rhem got his start, however, on the Clemson baseball team (1922–24). His major was engineering, but according to an article in the *Atlanta Constitution*, in truth, he majored in baseball, dropping out of college his junior year to sign with the Cardinals. When the "bashful and gawky" Rhem arrived at Clemson, he was well practiced at baseball, having played since the age of nine. At Clemson, he was a wonderful strikeout pitcher, gaining the name "Big Smoky." He later received the more permanent nickname "Shad" because of his Lowcountry fishing tales. Baseball scout Branch Rickey and others had great expectations for Rhem, who never fully lived up to them.[306]

Altogether, he spent twelve seasons in the majors, the best his 1926 season, when he won twenty games. Despite his ball-playing skills and some achievements, he was remembered best as a legendary and colorful character. In one pitching assignment, he asked for time and borrowed a trowel from the groundskeeper to reshape the pitcher's mound to his specifications.[307]

Rhem met and married Greer teacher Lula Dillard, and the couple retired to Greer after his career. He would have remembered the building of the Super Highway. The late Lula Dillard Rhem had mementos and great memories of train travel to ballgames across the East.[308] Greer relatives remember Flint Rhem in retirement cooking and eating one of his Lowcountry favorites, squirrel perlou, and going to his hunting cabin near his hometown of Rhems, South Carolina, named for his family and about twenty miles inland from Georgetown. In the Lowcountry, he fished from a boat on Black Mingo Creek and Swamp with a cane pole, a short line and a plug. His grandmother once owned land along the same creek where Francis Marion made an important crossing in September 1780 during the Revolutionary War and fought the Battle of Black Mingo.[309]

Both his accent and his love of hunting and fishing reflected his rural South Carolina Lowcountry roots. In Greer, he helped his wife sell sandwiches and snacks to peach-packers at Dillard's Peaches on South Buncombe Road. He died on July 30, 1969.[310] He is buried in Wood Memorial Park at the corner of Gap Creek Road and the Super Highway on the outskirts of Duncan. He was inducted into Clemson's Athletic Hall of Fame in 1979, and he received South Carolina's highest athletic honor when he was inducted posthumously into the South Carolina Athletic Hall of Fame on May 16, 2016.[311]

When it comes to colorful players, no one tops Rhem. Like some other players of his time, Rhem was known as one who loved whiskey. The best-known story is the time he didn't show up when he was scheduled to pitch for the Cardinals in a game against the Brooklyn Dodgers in Brooklyn. When he returned, Rhem claimed he was forced into a taxi by armed men (one version is that it was a group of armed Dodger fans) and made to drink whiskey—"awful stuff," he told his manager. His son, Sonny Rhem, now eighty-seven, in an interview with the *Post and Courier* (in Charleston), said, "He had an alcohol problem. It would come and go, come and go. He struggled with alcohol his entire life. That was his weakness.…My father was a very kind, gentle man. He would give you the shirt off his back; he was that kind of guy. While he had his problems, he made me a better person. I knew what I didn't want to be."[312]

Charles Flint Rhem. *Olivia Brittain-Toole, reference specialist, Special Collections and Archives, Clemson University.*

Other family members say much the same thing about Flint Rhem. They remember his knowledge of fishing and hunting, his tales of Babe Ruth and brothers Dizzy and Paul Dean, all members on various teams. They remember how he had peaches sent to Dizzy Dean during Dean's broadcasting years and was sometimes acknowledged on air by Dean as having received South Carolina peaches from his old buddy Flint Rhem. It would have been interesting to hear a conversation between Ruth and Rhem when they both played for the Boston Braves after Rhem had pitched against Ruth earlier with the Cardinals.[313]

Flint Rhem was "quite a character," as some would say. He was an excellent baseball player who traveled the country by train to play (before teams flew) and one who would have remembered the early years of the Super Highway.

White Oak (Waddell) Cemetery

The White Oak Cemetery (Waddell Family Cemetery) is an old monument-type cemetery. Many buried there, such as members of the Green, Raines, McCarter, Batson, West and other families, were among the first settlers of Greenville. White Oak Baptist Church and the cemetery were named after the stand of white oak trees growing there.

Isaac Green

Isaac Green, burried in the Waddell Cemetery (White Oak Baptist Church Cemetery) across from Bob Jones University, is not the most famous person buried near the Super Highway. Green's history, however, tells us much about the American Revolution and early Greenville County history. He was born in Mecklenburg County, North Carolina, on January 13, 1762, one of at least eight offspring of Joseph and Sarah McEntire Green in what became Tryon and later Cleveland County. He served as a Patriot with the South Carolina militia in the Revolutionary War, although his brother William Green fought for both sides and was with the British at the Battle of Kings Mountain. "Billy" Green later redeemed himself in the eyes of some by fighting for the Patriots at Eutaw Springs and later serving fourteen terms in the North Carolina Senate.[314] Significantly, his Patriot brother Isaac was part of an early migration to the South Carolina upcountry. As early as 1785, Isaac Green ahd received original land grants in what is now Greenville.[315]

A controversy over the naming of Greenville arises from Green's early settlement. Robert Mills thought the name came from the area's "verdant appearance."[316] A.S. Salley, secretary of the Historical Commission of South Carolina, wrote in 1946 that Greenville was named for "Isaac Green who

Early White Oak Baptist Church. *Courtesy of Nathan Majewski.*

ran a mill in Reedy River in which the town grew."[317] It is generally accepted today that Greenville was named after General Nathanael Greene, who commanded the Southern Campaign of the American Revolution. Dr. A.V. Huff Jr., former professor of history, vice president and dean at Furman University, writes, "The public records show that Isaac Green received his first land grant during the fall of 1785, and the legislative act naming the county passed March 22, 1786, less than six months after Isaac Green came into the country, and long before he built a mill on Reedy river."[318] Still another theory has it that Greenville was named after Elisha Greene, a wealthy landowner in the vicinity of the Isaac Green settlement.[319] It is easy to confuse the two seemingly unrelated Green families since they lived in the same area.

Significantly, the Isaac West family from Buffalo Creek, now Cleveland County, North Carolina, settled along Richland Creek, a tributary of the Reedy, and near the Green family.[320] Captain Isaac Green married Phoebe West, a daughter of Isaac West, Esq., in the year 1790 and settled near Mountain Creek. Phoebe West Green, interviewed for *Du Bow's Review* in 1853, spoke of living near the Battle of Kings Mountain and hearing shots from the battle and claimed that a Tory once struck her father on the head with a sword.[321]

Isaac and Phoebe West Green had eight children, six sons and two daughters. It is interesting that they named one son William, probably after his uncle who fought with the British at Kings Mountain.[322] Some progeny moved south and west to Texas and other states, but the name remains in Greenville County through their son Abraham and his sisters. Although a number of Greens/Greenes live in the Greenville area today, there are at least some descended from this pioneer family. Isaac and Phoebe West Green descendants are buried in the Waddell Cemetery, Woodlawn and other area cemeteries. Marriage placed the Greens among early Waddell and Raines

Above: White Oak Baptist Church collection plates. *Photo by Scott Withrow.*

Right: Isaac Green's gravestone. *Photo by Scott Withrow.*

families. In fact, family members lived in a home where Woodlawn Memorial Park is located today, and related Tolbert family members lived where Bob Jones University is located.[323]

By tradition, a member of the Waddell family gave land for White Oak Baptist Church, with the stipulation that white oak trees would remain bordering the property. Disease, however, required that some be cut, and someone with the church made collection plates out of some of the oak.[324] Many healthy-looking white oaks remain adjacent to the cemetery.

Chapter 9

BEAUTIFYING THE SUPER HIGHWAY AND REMEMBERING ITS LORE

In 1938, a beautification program was begun on the Super Highway. The announcement was made by F.E. Armstrong, who was the South Carolina State Highway Department's engineer for the western division. The cost was close to $20,000. Funding for the program was supplied by the Federal Bureau of Public Roads. The work was done on the first five miles of the Super Highway extending from Greenville to the road leading to Taylors. A workforce of forty men was tasked with the job of placing four thousand plants along the sides of the stretch of dual lanes.[325] Under the original plans for the Super Highway, grass was to be planted in the twenty-foot area between the dual lanes. United States Senator James F. Byrnes (a native of Spartanburg) asked officials of the federal Works Progress Administration in Washington, D.C., to join with the state highway department of South Carolina to plant crepe myrtle trees in this twenty-foot area.[326]

Walter Orlando "W.O." Ezell led a beautification program for Spartanburg that included a section of the route of the Super Highway at the Spartanburg end. After retiring as vice president and sales manager for the Geer Drug Company, Ezell began serving as the full-time chairman of the Spartanburg City Beautification Project. He had developed a love of flowers from an early age. In his work to beautify Spartanburg, Ezell helped establish more than 130 flower beds. Along the Spartanburg section of the Super Highway, he helped plant pansies, daffodils, crocuses and tulips, along with trees and shrubs. Ezell did much of the planting and tending to the flowers himself. He was supported by fellow members of the Spartanburg

Left: W.O. Ezell monument. *Photo by Scott Withrow.*

Right: W.O. Ezell. *Courtesy of Janet Wells Scarborough and Margaret Wells Hayslip. (Special thanks to Linda Tiller McHam.)*

Men's Garden Club.[327] This club was organized in 1948 by a group of men who wanted to share their interests in gardening. They became known as the Dirt Daubers.[328] Ezell shared daily gardening tips on Spartanburg radio station WSPA.[329] In 1968, in honor of Ezell's beautification work, the South Carolina Highway Commission changed the name of a two-mile stretch of the Super Highway in Spartanburg to W.O. Ezell Boulevard.[330]

The Dual Lane Highway and the Wrong Way Pilot

In 1938, Douglas Corrigan set a cross-country aviation record. He flew nonstop from California to New York in about twenty-seven hours in his single-engine 1929 Curtiss Robin airplane. After a layover in New York, Corrigan filed a flight plan to return to California and then took off from Floyd Bennett Field in New York. After a flight of just over twenty-eight hours, Douglas Corrigan landed at Baldonnel Airport in Dublin, Ireland. He told surprised officials that he had gotten lost and had not intended to fly to the east from New York. Corrigan said that he flew the wrong way because of a faulty compass and poor navigation that got him mixed up. His directional compass (N, S, E, W) failed, but his course compass (two needles to keep lined up) still worked. Corrigan followed the wrong end of the needle because he accidentally made a 360-degree turn instead of a 180-degree turn. He took off to the east and into the wind.[331] Corrigan returned to the United States from Ireland to a hero's welcome. He was given ticker tape parades and gifts such as compasses and backward running watches. He became known for the rest of his life as "Wrong Way" Corrigan.

In 1940, South Carolina had a pilot who flew the wrong way. He was a Furman University student who was also an aviation student. He had been flying solo and could not find the Greenville Municipal Airport. He recognized the dual lane (Super Highway) between Greenville and Spartanburg, so he landed his plane at what he believed to be the Greenville Airport. It turned out to be the Spartanburg Airport. He had followed the Super Highway the wrong way. Needless to say, there was no ticker tape parade waiting for him when he finally returned to Greenville.[332]

A SUPER HIGHWAY OR A WAGON ROAD?

Two very different types of wagons collided on the Super Highway in 1942. A wagon being pulled by a mule was rear ended by a station wagon. The wagon was demolished. The driver of the wagon and the driver of the station wagon survived, but the mule did not.[333]

PART III

THE SUPER HIGHWAY
TODAY

Chapter 10

THE FUTURE

Wade Hampton Boulevard in Greenville serves as a key connector between the city and suburbs and to Greer and beyond. One-third of traffic into Greenville is by way of Wade Hampton Boulevard. It is lined with businesses, but behind many of the businesses are neighborhoods. Throughout its length, it divides neighborhoods to the north and south.

In Greenville, planners with the city see danger to pedestrians and cyclists and seek to make the highway safer for both, as well as for drivers and passengers. Planners and administrators envision sidewalks that separate people further from traffic. Also under the plan, the city would encourage "higher quality economic investment." In total, the city would partner with the South Carolina State Department of Transportation "to create a safe environment for pedestrians and bicycles, add more greenspace, as well as slow down traffic and enhance the corridor."[334]

Slowing traffic would perhaps necessitate "road diets," the narrowing and channeling of traffic. The project could create roundabouts, realign intersections and create a shared path with a landscape buffer—in short, creating a Gateway to Greenville beginning in the area of Bob Jones University.[335] Wade Hampton Boulevard (the Super Highway) within the Greenville city limits would be replaced with a "super street."[336] Proponents of the project see the development of Northpoint Shopping Center as a catalyst for growth to an area they see as declining. They point to the fact that Highway 29 was once the main highway between Charlotte and Atlanta. They remember when that portion of Highway 29 was once thriving with such businesses as the Colonial Inn, Wade Hampton Mall, Carole's Record Shop and the Bijoux Theater.[337]

Others see this approach as gentrification, creating a zone of more expensive restaurants and other businesses to replace existing businesses (even some few remaining mom-and-pop businesses) and to impede and slow traffic flow—changes that go against traditional practices that have evolved with the use of the road. Some businesses fear they would have to change their signage, while others fear such a project might take their parking lot. Others fear a bike path would be unsafe for students attending area schools and that no sidewalk or path is completely safe where there is traffic. In essence, the highway would become more than a commuting highway.

Spartanburg also has plans for at least some of its portion of the Super Highway, especially West Main Street, envisioned as "a revitalized gateway to the city's downtown." Under this vision, the city would create an investment zone and a more pedestrian- and bike-friendly infrastructure, one that would enhance community pride. According to some, revitalization on this portion of the highway would help create a positive image for those entering the city.[338] Important to this section of the highway is the Coca-Cola Bottling Company building. Dating to 1936, the historic building reflects the architectural standards and Art Deco design of the Coca-Cola Bottling Company.[339] Plans are to repurpose the building for restaurant or retail space.[340]

Opposite: Coca-Cola Bottling Company, Spartanburg. *Photo by Scott Withrow.*

Above: Repurposed home, West Main, Spartanburg. *Photo by Scott Withrow.*

Left: Repurposed church, now Artists Collective. *Photo by Scott Withrow.*

Other West Main buildings have been repurposed. Perhaps one of the most interesting is a house now serving as an office that was once owned by an artist who gained notoriety in the 1930s for his lawn statues and carvings. One room of the bungalow-type house housed the artist's photography darkroom.[341] The present occupant thinks the house was built about 1927.

The Artists Collective is an interesting repurposed building, adding to a resurgence of West Main Street. It was at first a site for West Main Baptist Church, established in a tent on December 7, 1941 (Pearl Harbor Day), at its current location. Members arranged for a brick building soon thereafter and later added a front addition with a distinctive tower. It was no longer used as a church and vacant by 2008, and interested artists under the umbrella of the Spartanburg County Foundation established the Artists Cooperative with galleries, offices and workspace for artists. The name Main Street Baptist became Main Street Artists and then Main Street Cooperative.

Closer to Spartanburg and near the Southern Railway, Fifth Third Park will be the home for a professional baseball team affiliated with the Texas Rangers. The ballpark is planned to be state-of-the-art and serve also as an entertainment venue. Spartanburg last had a professional baseball team thirty years ago.[342]

Likewise, Spartanburg city officials and other stakeholders have worked to maximize Morgan Square's potential as a gathering place. Among other things, the project would create a dining zone adjacent to restaurants and "festival" streets adjoining the square (already completed to some extent). It would further pedestrianize the square.[343] Morgan Square as a gathering place dates to 1787, when it was known as the Public Square. It was designated Morgan Square in 1881 to celebrate the 100th anniversary of the Battle of Cowpens. Subsequently, Spartanburg erected a statue of General Daniel Morgan, the hero of the battle. The town clock, the Morgan statue and certain architecture are listed on the National Register of Historic Places.[344] Essentially, Morgan Square is the ending point of the Super Highway, at a point where Main Street begins.

proposal has nothing to do directly with the Super Highway. County others have proposed a high-speed rail line from Charlotte to three proposed routes, and one, the Southern Crescent, close to the Super Highway. Other, more expensive utes closer to I-85 and away from the Super whether high-speed rail would take some of the ighway.

Daniel Morgan statue, Morgan Square, Spartanburg. *Photo by Scott Withrow.*

Although it is easy to miss, a natural history endures along the Super Highway. The streams still flow, although many are now bridged, piped, channeled, culverted or diverted by parking lots and are perhaps more polluted than in the past. Many of the white oaks that are the namesake of White Oak Baptist Church and cemetery remain. Other trees remain, even a small forest on both sides of the highway near Chick Springs, near the North Tyger River in Spartanburg County, and at other places. And numerous subdivisions just off the Super Highway have trees. A series of generally north–south ridges at right angles to the highway are evident and make possible a view of Paris Mountain looking west from beyond Greer.

Whatever their view on the future, many have a love-hate relationship with the Super Highway. They love that it serves their travel and business interests, but they hate the traffic. They love its history, and some look back to its early days and a different era. There are many questions we can ask on its future, but it might be good to think about a national figure and proponent of superhighways. What would Dwight D. Eisenhower think about such superhighways and the interstate system today? What improvements would he make? In short, what would Ike do?

SOME SUPER HIGHWAY BUSINESSES

Spartanburg Area

A&B Aquarium
Warren H. Abernathy Highway, Clevedale (unincorporated)

Belk-Hudson Department Store
near Morgan Square, Spartanburg—the building still stands and is part of the Spartanburg Historic District, Morgan Square

Coca-Cola Bottling Company
500 West Main, Spartanburg—to be repurposed

Spartanburg Historic District
Buildings in and around Morgan Square

The Steeple Restaurant
W.O. Ezell Boulevard, Spartanburg—repurposed at one time as a used car dealership

Super Grille
Wellford, where the Super Highway once split

Wadsworth Pottery
Warren H. Abernathy Highway, Clevedale (unincorporated)

GREER-TAYLORS AREA

Adkins' Gulf Service
901 West Wade Hampton Boulevard, Greer

Belmont Drive-In Theatre
at the double bridges (twin bridges), Taylors

Ben Hughes Esso
Wade Hampton Boulevard, Greer

Benson's Auto
Super Highway, Greer

The Buttonwood Motel
corner of Wade Hampton Boulevard and St. Mark's Road, Taylors

Cloninger Motors
Ridgewood Drive and East Wade Hampton Boulevard, Greer

The Cotton Club
Wade Hampton Boulevard, Greer

Crate's Drive In
760 East Wade Hampton Boulevard, Greer

Culler-Jackson Furniture Company
Super Highway, Greer-Duncan area—repurposed for a number of businesses

Dairy Queen Brazier
1301 West Wade Hampton Boulevard, Greer

Dewey Harrison Gulf Service Station
Wade Hampton Boulevard, Greer

Dill's Miniature Golf Course
Wade Hampton Boulevard, Greer

Don Edward's Dual Lane Shell
Super Highway and Appalache Crossing, Greer

Don's Dual Lane Auto Auction
Super Highway and Appalache Crossing

El Matador Restaurant
2919 Wade Hampton Boulevard, Taylors—longtime Mexican restaurant

The Flour Barrel
East Wade Hampton Boulevard, Greer

The Fork Restaurant
1165 West Wade Hampton Boulevard, Greer (parking lot adjacent to the Super Highway)
1406 West Poinsett Street, Greer (parking lots adjacent to Poinsett Street)

Harley Bonds Furniture
109 West Wade Hampton Boulevard Greer
Hart's Gulf Station
101 West Wade Hampton Boulevard, Greer
Hightower Oil Company
West Wade Hampton Boulevard, Greer
Hillcrest Memorial Gardens
14050 East Wade Hampton Boulevard, Greer
The Holiday Motel
East Wade Hampton Boulevard, near Appalache Crossing, Greer
Horton's Restaurant
advertised as between Taylors and Greer on Wade Hampton Boulevard—later Teamster's Union building (Horton's was not far from Norton's)
Hubert Coggin's Amoco Station
Super Highway, Greer
King Cotton Drive-In Theater
off Super Highway near the Appalache Crossing, Greer—repurposed for a time as a flea market
Lonnie's Sinclair
Wade Hampton Boulevard, Greer
Mayfair Restaurant
1312 West Wade Hampton Boulevard, Greer—meat and three
Norton's Restaurant
owned by Faye Norton, in a mobile home, aka the Dinky Diner, 5330 Wade Hampton Boulevard, between Main Street and Old Rutherford Road, Taylors
Open-Hearth Restaurant
2801 Wade Hampton Boulevard, Taylors—well known for many years, especially for functions
Palmetto State Oil Company
614 East Wade Hampton Boulevard, Greer
The Peach Bowl
(12 AMF Automatic Pin Spotters), East Spartanburg Highway (Wade Hampton Boulevard)
Pete's Restaurant
14155 East Wade Hampton Boulevard, Greer
Po Folks Restaurant
1108 West Wade Hampton Boulevard, Greer

Skyline Motor Court
  Skyline Drive and Wade Hampton Boulevard, Taylors
Super Highway Oil Company
  Wade Hampton Boulevard, Greer
Tab's Dairy Bar
  1333 West Wade Hampton Boulevard, Greer
Tab's Flea Market
  East Wade Hampton Boulevard, Greer, near the South Tyger River
Tic Toc Drive In
  1107 West Wade Hampton Boulevard, Greer
Wade Hampton Esso Service Station
  Wade Hampton Boulevard and Arlington Road, Appalache Crossing, Greer
Wade Hampton Motel
  Wade Hampton Boulevard, Taylors (the owner was Wade Hampton Greene; some say Greene named it after himself)
The Wayfarer Steak House
  2611 Wade Hampton Boulevard (1½ miles beyond Liberty Life on left, Highway 29 North)
The Weiner King
  700 East Wade Hampton Boulevard, Greer
Wingo's Motel
  Wade Hampton Boulevard—the building still stands across from Dobson's Gifts and Hardware
Wood Memorial Park
  863 Gap Creek Road, in sight of the Super Highway, Greer
W.W. Mason Motor Company
  Super Highway, Greer

Greenville Area

Benson's Shell Station
  one and a half miles from Greer on the Super Highway, Benson's sold electric ranges by Hot Point, oil heaters by Coleman and Evans and refrigerators by Admiral
Bonny's Drive-In Restaurant
  located on the Super Highway at Earle Street in Greenville; specialized in steaks, southern fried chicken, country ham and seafood

Carole's Record Shop

641 Wade Hampton Boulevard, Greenville (see also Wade Hampton Mall)

Craig-Rush Furniture Company

located on the Super Highway near Bob Jones University

El Rancho Café

located across from the Belmont Drive-In Theatre; Herman Affalter was the manager

Homer's Gulf Station

300 East Stone Avenue, Greenville; at one time it was the Super Highway Service Station (Gulf), also a used car dealership, now the Universal Joint Bar and Grill

McBride's Office Supply

Wade Hampton Boulevard, Greenville

Rimer Incorporated, "The Place with the Up Side Down Sign"

located on the Super Highway across from the Belmont Drive-In Theatre; it had five acres of mobile homes, a furniture store, trailer parts store and general insurance agency

Scruggs Equipment Co., Inc.

sold hotel, restaurant, store and butcher supplies, as well as commercial refrigerator equipment

Sears Roebuck Company

located where the Super Highway began in Greenville

Super Highway Service Station

see Homer's Gulf Station and Universal Joint Bar and Grill

Super Supply Company (Greenville)

sold air condition units made by Philco for home and office

Universal Joint Bar and Grill

see Homer's Gulf Station and Super Highway Service Station

Wade Hampton Mall

The Wade Hampton Mall on the Super Highway saw the opening of its first store on November 1, 1962. W.T. Grant's doors opened to customers on that date. By 1964, there were fourteen additional businesses at the mall, plus two professional offices. The Wade Hampton Mall was advertised as "Greenville's Friendliest Shopping Center," with over one thousand free parking spaces. W.T. Grant's thirty-thousand-square-foot department store was the anchor business. Grant's sold a wide variety of items that included clothes, record albums, stamp collecting kits, stamp packets and baby chicks (in the spring).

The *Greenville News* published a supplement in 1970 telling people where fallout shelters were located in Greenville to be used in the event of a nuclear attack. Eight businesses at the Wade Hampton Mall were on the list, including W.T. Grant department store. Today, the property where the Wade Hampton Mall was located is owned by Bob Jones University.

Wade Hampton Mall Businesses—1964

Carole's Record & Hi-Fi Shop (later 641 Wade Hampton Boulevard, Greenville)

Draughan's Business College

Economy Auto Stores

Ko Ko Tee Beauty Salon

Lees-Wright

Mall Cleaners

Orvin Barber Shop

The Peoples National Bank

Perry's Casual Shop

Phillips Jewelry & Gifts

Rutz Shoe Repair

Wade Hampton Pet Center

Walgreens

Winn-Dixie Stores

W.T. Grant Co.

NOTES

Chapter 1

1. Chapman J. Milling, *Red Carolinians* (Chapel Hill, NC: University of North Carolina Press, 1940), 231–32.
2. "Deerskin Trade," *South Carolina Encyclopedia*, www.scencyclopedia.org/sce/entries/deerskin-trade.
3. Verner W. Crane, *The Southern Frontier, 1670–1732* (Durham, NC: Duke University Press, 1928), 110–12.
4. Michael Trinkley, Debi Hacker and Natalie Adams, "A Preliminary Archaeological Context for Greenville County, South Carolina," *Chicora Foundation* 21, www.chicora.org/pdfs/Greenville%20Context.pdf.
5. Ibid., 1–7.
6. "Topper Site," *University of South Carolina Salkehatchie*, sc.edu/about/system_and_campuses/salkehatchie/community/topper_site/index.php#:~:text=The%20Topper%20Site%20is%20the,be%20fifty%20thousand%20years%20old.
7. Lewis P. Jones, *South Carolina: One of the Fifty States* (Orangeburg, SC: Sandlapper Publishing, Inc., 1985), 272–74.
8. Louis De Vorsey Jr., *Indian Boundaries in the Southern Colonies, 1763–1775* (Chapel Hill: University of North Carolina Press, 1966), 98–109; James M. Richardson, *History of Greenville County, South Carolina, Narrative and Biographical* (Spartanburg, SC: Preprint Company, 1980; originally published in Atlanta, 1930), 41.

9. For example, see "Plat Map of Abraham Mayfield's Land Survey of Greenville County, S.C., Performed on 18 Oct. 1791," *Mayfields of South Carolina*, mayfieldsofsc.tripod.com/plat_map.htm; "But It Never Was," *Greenville News*, April 11, 1937, 23, www.newspapers.com/newspage/188033529.

10. Archie Vernon Huff, *Greenville: The History of the City and County in the South Carolina Piedmont* (Columbia: University of South Carolina Press), 1995, 13–18.

11. Carole Watterson Troxler, "Refuge, Resistance, and Reward: The Southern Loyalists' Claim on East Florida," *Journal of Southern History* 55 (November 1989): 563–96; Mildred Whitmire, "Richard Pearis: Saint or Sinner," *Greenville News*, June 26, 1962, 8A, www.newspapers.com/image/189051887/?clipping_id=6448878&fcfToken=eyJhbGciOiJIUzI1NiIsInR5cCI6Ikp XVCJ9. eyJmcmVlLXZpZXctaWQiOjE4OTA1MTg4NywiaWF0IjoxNzEwEwODA1N jk1LCJleHAiOjE3MTA4OTIwOTV9.JScAGnHh96b GOR-pqLA06cPsnTfFuhWYreFyTpXo3Bo.

12. Huff, *Greenville*, 14, 17–18; Whitmire, "Pearis," 4.

13. De Vorsey, *Indian Boundaries in the Southern Colonies*, 102.

14. Susan Dixon, "The Hampton Massacre," *The State*, June 30, 1940, dspace. ychistory.org/server/api/core/bitstreams/950e13fc-576f-40f6-bf44-75f3a1b806a3/content.

15. John Belton O'Neall Landrum, *Colonial and Revolutionary History of Upper South Carolina* (Greenville, SC: Shannon and Company Printers and Binders, 1897), 86–89, www.carolana.com/SC/eBooks/Colonial_and_Revolutionary_History_of_Upper_South_Carolina_J_B_O_Landrum.pdf.

16. USC–Lancaster Native-American Studies Center, F. Evan Nooe (lecture), "Making the Hampton Massacre: Native Resistance, Settler Memory, and White Solidarity in South Carolina," *South Carolina Living*, April 19, 2022, www.scliving.coop; F. Evan Nooe, *Aggressions and Sufferings: Settler Violence, Native Resistance, and Coalescence of the Old South* (Tuscaloosa: University of Alabama Press, 2023), 169–76.

17. "Hampton," Historical Marker Database, www.hmdb.org/m.asp?m=10400.

18. "Early White Settlement: The Massacre of Jacob Hite," Historical Marker Database, www.hmdb.org/m.asp?m=24254.

19. "Woods Fort," Historical Marker Database, www.hmdb.org/m.asp?m=10398.

20. Ray Belcher and Joada P. Hiatt, *Greer: From Cotton Town to Industrial Center* (Charleston, SC: Arcadia Publishing, 2003), 13–14.

21. Mann Batson, *Early Travel and Accommodations Along the Roads of the Upper Part of Greenville County, South Carolina* (Travelers Rest, SC: Mann Batson, 1995), 1.

22. Anne K. McCuen, *Including a Pile of Rocks* (Greenville, SC: Southern Historical Press, Inc, 2005), 122–33.

23. Batson, *Early Travel and Accommodations*, 1.

24. "Indian Boundary Line," Historical Marker Database, www.hmdb.org/m.
asp?m=11264.

25. Caroline S. Coleman, "Old Indian Boundary Line Be Marked by Greer DAR
Chapter," *Greenville Piedmont*, May 2, 1952, 15. Thanks to staff in the South
Carolina Room, Greenville County Library, for locating the source of the article.

Chapter 2

26. Batson, *Early Travel and Accommodations*, 156, citing *Southern Patriot*, August 10,
1854.

27. Jean Martin Flynn, *An Account of Taylors, South Carolina, 1817–1994*
(Spartanburg, SC: Reprint Company, Publishers, 1995), 159–61.

28. Dr. A.V. Huff, personal correspondence, January 26, 2024; see also Flynn,
Taylors, 161; Theresa M. Hicks and Wes Taukchiray, eds., *South Carolina Indians,
Indian Traders and Other Ethnic Connections Beginning in 1670* (Spartanburg, SC:
Reprint Company, Publishers, 1998), 65–66. Hicks and Taukchiray list twenty-
seven Catawba Indians in Greenville County in 1849. It is not certain whether
all Catawba were included, especially those intermarried with whites.

29. David J. Cranford, R.P. Stephen Davis Jr., Theresa McReynolds Shebalin and
Brett H. Riggs, "Adoption and Use of Log Cabins in the Catawba Nation, c.
1759–1820," in *Native American Log Cabins in the Southeast*, edited by Gregory A.
Waselkov (Knoxville: University of Tennessee Press, 2019), 67–87.

30. Robert Mills, *Statistics of South Carolina* (Charleston, SC: Hurlburt & Lloyd,
1826), 48; see also Jean Martin Flynn, "Chick Springs 1840–1941," *Proceedings
and Papers of the Greenville County Historical Society* 6 (1981): 40.

31. Copy of the analysis provided by Fred Bagwell.

32. "Medicine and Miracles: The Chemistry of Spring Waters," chapter 3
in Francis H. Chapelle, *Wellspring: A Natural History of Bottled Spring Waters*
(Piscataway, NJ: Rutgers University Press, 2005), 41–61; "Chick Springs Health
Resort (advertisement)," *Greenville News*, January 29, 1928, www.newspapers.
com/image/188232770/?clipping_id=9591448&fcfToken=eyJhbGciOiJIUzI1
NiIsInR5cCI6IkpXVCJ9.eyJmcmVlLXZpZXctaWQiOjE4ODIzMjc3MCwia
WF0IjoxNzA2NzQ3NDA0LCJleHAiOjE3MDY4MzM4MDR9.2SV4D07pD6
GqjFcGprjfq6iGUxCkSLX-H9FFG5bqWK0.

33. Thomas A. Chambers, *Drinking the Waters: Creating an American Leisure Class at
Nineteenth Century Mineral Springs* (Washington, D.C.: Smithsonian Institution
Press, 2002), 28–30, 64–65.

34. Mary F. Fanslow, "Resorts in Southern Appalachia: A Microcosm of American Resorts in the Nineteenth and Early Twentieth Centuries," thesis, East Tennessee State University, dc.etsu.edu/cgi/viewcontent. cgi?article=2118&context=etd.

35. Flynn, "Chick Springs," 41 citing *Greenville Mountaineer*, May 27, 1842.

36. Chambers, *Drinking the Waters*, 85; see also Jean Martin Flynn, *History of the First Baptist Church of Taylors, S.C.* (Clinton, SC: Jacobs Brothers, 1964), 10.

37. "Chick Springs: The South's Peerless Summer and Health Resort," *Union Times*, July 27, 1906, 3, chroniclingamerica.loc.gov/lccn/sn93067853/1906-07-27/ ed-1/seq-3/#date1=1882&sort=relevance&rows=20&words=Chick+Springs&se archType=basic&sequence=0&index=7&state=South+Carolina&date2=1963&p roxtext=Chick+springs&y=14&x=15&dateFilterType=yearRange&page=2.

38. Melissa Walker, "Mineral Waters, Dancing, and Amusements: The Development of Tourism in the Nineteenth-Century Upcountry South Carolina History," in *Recovering the Piedmont Past: Unexplored Moments in Nineteenth-Century Upcountry South Carolina History*, edited by Timothy P. Grady and Melissa Walker (Columbia: University of South Carolina Press, 2013), 12.

39. Flynn, *Taylors*, 1–7.

40. Jeremiah Joseph O'Connell, *Catholicity in the Carolinas and Georgia: Leaves of Its History* (New York: D. and J. Sadlier and Co., 1879), 368–70.

41. Ibid., 370.

42. Walker, "Mineral Waters," 12.

43. Flynn, *Taylors*, 43.

44. Huff, *Greenville*, 112–14.

45. Flynn, *Taylors*, 6; Flynn, "Chick Springs," 44–45; Flynn, *History of the First Baptist Church*, 16–17, 28.

46. Flynn, "Chick Springs," 46–47.

47. Greer (SC) Heritage Museum, unidentified newspaper clipping, Grace Wells Taylor, "Chick Springs History: Newberry Doctor Was to See Future in Locality," July 31, 1947.

48. *Union Times*, August 31, 1906, 3, chroniclingamerica.loc.gov/lccn/ sn93067853/1906-08-31/ed-1/seq-3/#date1=1896&index=14&rows=20&wor ds=Chick+CHICK+SPRING+Springs&searchType=basic&sequence=0&state =South+Carolina&date2=1906&proxtext=chick+springs&y=14&x=20&dateFi lterType=yearRange&page=1.

49. Flynn, *Taylors*, 155–56.

50. "Chick Springs Hotel (advertisement)," *Greenville News*, May 31, 1918 www. newspapers.com/image/188082182/?terms=chick%20springs%20hotel%20 &match=1.

51. "Chick Springs Proving Popular Resort," *Greenville News*, June 19, 1918, 6, https://www.newspapers.com/image/188085130/?terms=chick%20springs%20proving%20&match=1.

52. Flynn, *Taylors*, 156–57.

53. Ibid., 158.

54. Ibid., 156–57; "Little 'Coney Island' Being Constructed at Chick Springs Resort Few Miles from the City," *Greenville News*, May 13, 1929, 10, www.newspapers.com/image/229044989/?terms=little%20coney%20island&match=1.

55. Fred Bagwell, interview with the author, August 8, 2023. Fred Bagwell has in his possession a copy of the letter.

56. "Water Company Suing Highway Department," *Greenville News*, February 6, 1936.

57. Flynn, *Taylors*, 163–64.

58. Paul Green, interview with the author.

59. Buddy Bowman, *Running Barefoot Through the Southern Piedmont* (Buddy Bowman, 2023), 42–43.

60. Margaret S. Bull Obituary, *Greenville News*, October 29, 1993, 29, www.newspapers.com/image/192466718/?match=1&terms=margaret%20sloan%20bull.

61. Green, interview with the author.

62. Flynn, *Taylors*, 164.

63. Ibid., 158.

64. "Chick Springs," Taylors Town Square, www.taylorstownsquare.com/chick-springs.

Chapter 3

65. Spartanburg Unit of the Writers' Program of the Works Progress Administration in the State of South Carolina, comp., *A History of Spartanburg County* (1940), 273–74.

66. Thomas T. Fetters, *The Piedmont and Northern: The Great Electric System of the South* (San Marino, CA: Golden West Books, 1974), 95.

67. Writers' Program of the Works Progress Administration, *History of Spartanburg County*.

68. Constance H. Dillard, *Of Days and Times Remembered*, privately printed, 1977.

69. Fetters, *Piedmont and Northern*, 95.

70. Ibid., 101.

71. Ibid., 103.

72. Writers' Program of the Works Progress Administration, *History of Spartanburg County*, 277.

73. Craig Myers, "A Peach of a Story," *TIES magazine*, September–October 2005, 4–5.
74. Lemuel Dillard, interview with the author, June 27, 2024.
75. Myers, "Peach of a Story."
76. C.V. "Mac" McMillin, "Recollections of the Son of a Grower," *TIES magazine*, September–October 2005, 15.

Chapter 4

77. "A Brief History of Camp Sevier," www.greenville.k12.sc.us/sevier/Upload/Uploads/Brief%20History%20of%20Camp%20Sevier.pdf.
78. *Greenville News*, September 30, 1917.
79. *Greenville News*, October 27, 1917.
80. *Greenville News*, October 5, 1917.
81. *Camp Sevier Completion Report*, 1918 (courtesy of Bob Dicey's Camp Sevier collection).
82. Tent and Trench, schistory.net/campwadsworth.
83. "Twenty-Seventh Infantry Division (United States)," Wikipedia, en.wikipedia.org/wiki/27th_Infantry_Division_(United_States)#History
84. *The Sun* (NY), September 17, 1917.

Chapter 5

85. Ernest Everett Blevins, email correspondence, June 18, 2024. Ernest Everett Blevins is one of the most—if not the most—knowledgeable persons on the Bankhead and National Highways in South Carolina. Also, Ernest Everett Blevins, "The Bankhead Highway in Spartanburg: The World's Longest Highway Bisects the County," poster courtesy of Brad Steinecke, director of Local History, Kennedy Room, Headquarters, Spartanburg County Library.
86. Dan L. Smith, *Texas Highway No. 1: The Bankhead Highway in Texas—A History and Driving Guide for the Nation's Earliest All-Weather Transcontinental Highway* (Fort Worth, TX: Bankhead Highway Publishing, 2013).
87. "National Highway," Historical Marker Database, www.hmdb.org/m.asp?m=198225.
88. Richard F. Weingroff, "The Lincoln Highway," U.S. Department of Transportation, Federal Highway Administration, highways.dot.gov/highway-history/general-highway-history/lincoln-highway; see also Brandon K.

Hardison, "Automotive History—January 16, 1916—The Federal Highway Act," LinkedIn/Pulse/Automotive History, www.linkedin.com/pulse/automotive-history-january-16-1916-federal-highway-act-hardison.

89. Ronald W. Edrich, "The 'Broadway of America' Connected the South," *Austin American-Statesman*, September 26, 2018, www.statesman.com/story/news/2016/09/24/the-broadway-of-america-connected-the-south/9864043007.

90. T. Lindsay Baker, "Eating Up Route 66: Foodways on America's Mother Road," online speaker, Center for Texas Studies at TCU, January 6, 2024.

91. "The Bankhead Highway: Broadway of America," Preserving Texas History, freepages.rootsweb.com/~unclejoe/history/tx/bankhead.html.

92. Rickie Longfellow, "Route 66: The Mother Road," Federal Highway Administration, Highway History, www.fhwa.dot.gov/infrastructure/back0303.cfm.

93. Martin T. Olliff, *Getting Out of the Mud: The Alabama Good Roads Movement and Highway Administration, 1898–1928* (Tuscaloosa: University of Alabama Press, 2017), 3.

94. Howard Lawrence Preston, *Dirt Roads to Dixie: Accessibility and Modernization in the South, 1885–1935* (Knoxville: University of Tennessee Press, 1991), 12–13, 95–96.

95. "Road Race Through Greer," Greer Heritage Museum, www.greerheritage.com/2020/01/19/greer-road-race.

96. Preston, *Dirt Roads to Dixie*, 33–36.

97. "John Hollis Bankhead," Encyclopedia of Alabama, encyclopediaofalabama.org/article/john-hollis-bankhead.

98. "United States Good Roads Association," *Southern Good Roads*, May 1917, 10, digital.ncdcr.gov/Documents/Detail/southern-good-roads-1917-may/478206?item=580414.

99. "Captain John Henry Brockman," Find a Grave, www.findagrave.com/memorial/36715962/james_henry_brockman.

100. "John Asa Rountree," Encyclopedia of Alabama, encyclopediaofalabama.org/media/john-asa-rountree.

101. Leo Landis, "Thomas Harris MacDonald," Iowa State University Biographical Dictionary, isubios.pubpub.org/pub/ctpiloqc/release/1.

102. Tom Lewis, *Divided Highways: Building the Interstate Highways, Transforming American Life* (New York: Penguin Publishing Group, 1999), 8–15.

103. Olliff, *Getting Out of the Mud*, 6–7.

104. Ibid., 6.

105. Andrew Nelson Lytle, "The Hind Tit," in *I'll Take My Stand* (Baton Rouge: Louisiana State University Press, 1977), 234–40; originally published New York: Harper and Brothers, 1930.

106. *Southern Good Roads*, August 1919, 9.

107. Preston, *Dirt Roads to Dixie*, 20–21.

108. *Southern Good Roads*, May 1917, 9.

109. Olliff, *Getting Out of the Mud*, 5–6.

110. "Cotton Tom's Last Blast, April 26, 1932," United States Senate, www.senate. gov/artandhistory/history/minute/Cotton_Toms_Last_Blast.htm.

111. "No Federal Aid for This State," *Greenville News*, March 30, 1916, www. newspapers.com/image/187854448/?terms=No%20Federal%20Aid%20 for%20this%20state&match=1.

112. John Hammond Moore, *The South Carolina Highway Department, 1917–1987* (Columbia: University of South Carolina Press, 1987), 49–52.

113. Texas Historical Commission, "The Development of Highways in Texas: A Historic Context of the Bankhead Highway and Other Historic Named Highways," www.thc.texas.gov/public/upload/preserve/survey/highway/ Section%20I.%20Statewide%20Historic%20Context.pdf; David Banasiak, "Origins of the Interstates," *Roads and Bridges*, December 28, 2000, www. roadsbridges.com/asphalt/interstate-system/article/10581849/origins-of-the-interstates.

114. Donna Isbell Walker, "100 Years Ago Camp Sevier in Greenville Played Key Role in Fighting, Ending World War I," *Greenville News*, January 18, 2018, www.greenvilleonline.com/story/entertainment/2018/01/18/camp-sevier-greenville-played-critical-role-s-100th-anniversary-commemorated-remember-old-hickory-pr/1043588001.

115. Karl Raitz, "American Roads—Roadside America," *Geographical Review* 88, no. 3 (1998): 363, 378.

116. Preston, *Dirt Roads to Dixie*, 115.

117. Dot Arms, interview with the author, November 15, 2023.

118. Betsy Wakefield Teter, Karen Nutt and Bill Lynch, "Pacific Mills" (Textile Town Appendix), in *Textile Town: Spartanburg County, South Carolina*, edited by Betsy Wakefield Teter (Spartanburg, SC: Hub City Writers Project, 2012), 313.

119. Owner, Red Hill Hot Dogs, communication with the author, April 28, 2024.

120. Staff writer, *Herald Journal*, "Who Was Florence Chapel," *Go Upstate*, September 17, 2003, www.goupstate.com/story/news/2003/09/17/who-was-florence-chapel/29683601007; "Sunny Graded School," City of Wellford, www.cityofwellford.com/about.html.

121. Major John F. Fairchild, "Map of Camp Wadsworth (May 2, 1918)," courtesy of Brad Steinecke, assistant director of local history, Kennedy Room, Headquarters Library, Spartanburg County Public Library.

122. Linda Conley, "Camp Wadsworth," *Go Upstate*, January 23, 2002, www.goupstate.com/story/news/2002/07/23/camp-wadsworth/29645523007.

123. Susan Thoms, "Surviving Camp Wadsworth: Health Issues Confront Local Soldiers," in *When the Soldiers Came to Town: Spartanburg's Camp Wadsworth (1917–1919) and Camp Croft (1941–45)*, edited by Susan Turpin, Carolyn Creal, Ron Crawley and James Crocker (Spartanburg, SC: Hub City Writers Project, 2004), 46.

124. "Spartanburg One of the Leading Cities of the South Carolina Piedmont," *Greenville News*, October 19, 1930, www.newspapers.com/image/191634681/?terms=National%20highway&match=1.

125. Flynn, *History of the First Baptist Church*, 16–27.

126. Jeanie Putnam, "The Evolution of the Southern Bleachery and Print Works," *Greenville News*, February 28, 2020, 18, www.newspapers.com/image/879514095/?terms=taylors%20mill&match=1.

127. Richard Weingroff, "Zero Milestone—Washington, D.C.," U.S. Department of Transportation, Federal Highway Administration, highways.dot.gov/highway-history/general-highway-history/zero-milestone-washington-dc.

128. J.A. Rountree Journal (excerpt), provided by Martin T. Olliff communication with the author, May 18, 2023.

129. Weingroff, "Zero Milestone."

130. "Greenville Roads Best Passed Over Highway Men Say," *Greenville News*, June 27, 1920, www.newspapers.com/image/187959970/?terms=bankhead%20convoy&match=1.

131. Maureen McGee, "Vintage Military Vehicles Re-enact 1920 Convoy," *San Diego Union-Tribune*, October 17, 2015, www.sandiegouniontribune.com/2015/10/17/vintage-military-vehicles-re-enact-1920-convoy.

132. Tom Taylor, "Spirit of '45 Military Vehicles on the Bankhead Highway," Random Connections, September 27, 2015, www.randomconnections.com/spirit-of-45-military-vehicles-on-the-bankhead-highway/#more-10384.

133. Walker, "100 Years Ago Camp Sevier."

134. "Rosemond, James R.," South Carolina Encyclopedia, www.scencyclopedia.org/sce/entries/rosemond-james-r.

135. "Silver Hill—Spartanburg's Oldest African-American Methodist Church," Wofford Blogs (Wofford.edu), blogs.wofford.edu/from_the_archives/2008/02/08/silver-hill-s.

136. "Charters and Commissions," *Greenville News*, February 4, 1911, 2, www.newspapers.com/image/188088014/?match=1&terms=Greenville%20Nursery%20company.

137. "Evergreens! Evergreens!" *Greenville News*, January 21, 1920, 7, www.newspapers.com/image/188204381/?terms=greenville%20nursery%20incorporated&match=1.

138. "For Sale: Shrubbery, Evergreens, Roses, and Fruit Trees," *Greenville News*, January 6, 1924, 22, www.newspapers.com/image/188214711/?terms=greenville%20nursery&match=1.

139. "Nursery Making Rapid Progress," *Greenville News*, December 7, 1924, 12, www.newspapers.com/image/188214279/?match=1&terms=Greenville%20Nursery%20company.

140. "Shuttle Constriction," Greenville County Library System, greenvillelibrary.contentdm.oclc.org/digital/collection/p17168coll60/id/12/rec/9.

141. "Heddle," Merriam-Webster, www.merriam-webster.com/dictionary/heddle.

142. "Heddle Hill (About Us)," heddlehill.com/about-us.

143. Ibid.

144. Amy Clarke Burns, "QandAmy: Something New at the Old Steel Heddle," *Greenville News*, March 20, 2015, www.greenvilleonline.com/story/news/local/2015/03/19/qamy-something-new-old-steel-heddle/25035385.

145. "Southern Worsted Corporation," *Greenville News*, April 17, 1923, 9, www.newspapers.com/image/188222964/?terms=southern%20worsted&match=1; "Bennette Eugene Geer '96, (1933–1938): Overview," Special Collections and Archives, Furman University, libguides.furman.edu/special-collections/bennette-geer.

146. "First Woolen Cloth Woven in South Last Week at Plant of Southern Worsted Corporation," *Greenville News*, May 12, 1924, 5, www.newspapers.com/image/188175681/?terms=southern%20worsted%20men%27s%20suits&match=1.

147. "12 South Carolina Firms Given 14 War Contracts," *Greenville News*, December 22, 1940, 6, www.newspapers.com/image/187722586/?terms=southern%20worsted%20army%20cloth&match=1.

148. "Plant to Be in Operation by February—Mill Village Ready for Occupancy," *Charlotte Observer*, January 11, 1924, 2, www.newspapers.com/image/616504908/?terms=southern%20worsted%20mill%20village&match=1.

149. "Contract Let for Huge Mill," *Greenville News*, June 29, 1923, 1, www.newspapers.com/image/188204906/?terms=%20to%20Build%20southern%20worsted%20&match=1.

150. "Minter Homes," West Virginia Encyclopedia, www.wvencyclopedia.org/articles/2001.

151. "World's Largest Housing Factor Opens Huge Plant in the South," *Greenville News*, May 30, 1920, 23, www.newspapers.com/image/187958524/?terms=minter%20homes&match=1.

152. Mike Reynolds, interview with the author, March 28, 2024.

153. "Cities Service ad," *Greenville News*, October 10, 1954, 11, www.newspapers.com/image/191627867/?terms=fleming%20grocery&match=1.

154. "Private Meeting Among Pastors Paves Way for Taylors Church," *Greenville News*, August 29, 2000, 45, www.newspapers.com/image/194534366/?terms=pebble%20creek%20southern%20worsted&match=1.

155. Reynolds interview.

156. Jeff Mace, interview with the author, March 25, 2024.

157. "History of Shriners Children's Greenville," www.shrinerschildrens.org/en/locations/greenville/about-us/our-history.

158. "Herdklotz Park," Visit Greenville, www.visitgreenvillesc.com/listing/herdklotz-park/6244.

159. Randy Mallory, "Original Texas Road Trip: Tracing History Along the Bankhead Highway," Texas Highways, October 17, 2020, texashighways.com/culture/original-texas-road-trip-bankhead-highway.

160. "Mark Bankhead Highway Route," *Greenville News*, June 18, 1920, 3, www.newspapers.com/image/187959460/?match=1&terms=Mark%20Bankhead%20Highway%20Route.

161. William (Trogdon) Least Heat-Moon, *Blue Highways: A Journey into America* (Boston: Little, Brown, and Company, 1982).

Chapter 6

162. Benton MacKaye and Lewis Mumford, "Townless Highways for the Motorist: A Proposal for the Automobile Age," *Harper's Magazine*, August 1, 1931, 347–56.

163. Lewis, *Divided Highways*, 51.

164. Ibid.

165. Teal Arcadi, "Partisanship and Permanence: How Congress Contested the Origins of the Interstate Highway System and the Future of American Infrastructure," Cambridge University Press, April 1, 2022, www.cambridge.org/core/journals/modern-american-history/article/partisanship-and-permanence-how-congress-contested-the-origins-of-the-interstate-highway-system-and-the-future-of-american-infrastructure/39B009B-9DE542D9B36EC254FB79DE542; Maxwell Prime, "Working Hard or Hardly

Working:? An Examination of Work Relief Programs in Upstate New York, 1931–1943," Union College Digital Works, June 2014, digitalworks.union.edu/cgi/viewcontent.cgi?article=1584&context=theses.

166. "New Greenville-Spartanburg Super-Highway Likely to Be Started in 10 Days," *Greenville News*, June 7, 1936, www.newspapers.com/image/188666911/?terms=super%20highway&match=1; "Acton Is Taken to Bring About Complete Paving of Super Highway," *Greenville News*, May 8, 1943, 3, www.newspapers.com/image/187955867/?match=1.

167. "$2,000,000 Super Highway Between Greenville, Spartanburg Planned," *Greenville News*, June 18, 1935, 2, www.newspapers.com/image/188482699/?terms=super%20highway&match=1.

168. "Seeks Cooperation," *Greenville News*, August 1, 1935, 14, www.newspapers.com/image/188280827/?terms=seeks%20cooperation&match=1.

169. Thomas Hughes, interview with the author, October 5, 2023.

170. Lewis, *Divided Highways*, xiii.

171. "$2,000,000 Super Highway Planned," 2.

172. Paul Green, interview with the author, November 15, 2023.

173. "Work Starts Today on Spartan Highway," *Greenville News*, June 26, 1936, 6, www.newspapers.com/image/188667359/?terms=%20E.%20W.%20Grannis%20of%20Fayetteville%2C%20North%20Carolina&match=1.

174. "Highway Department to Ask Bids at Once of Super Highway," *Greenville News*, May 2, 1936, 1, www.newspapers.com/image/188667359/?terms=%20E.%20W.%20Grannis%20of%20Fayetteville%2C%20North%20Carolina&match=1.

175. *Greenville News*, June 26, 1936, 6.

176. *Greenville News*, June 7, 1936, 2.

177. *Greenville News*, June 26, 1936, 6.

178. *Greenville News*, August 23, 1936, 7.

179. *Greenville News*, September 29, 1938, 3.

180. "Herbert E. Wolfe," Wikipedia, en.wikipedia.org/wiki/Herbert_E._Wolfe.

181. *Greenville News*, August 1, 1945, 10.

182. *The State*, March 15, 1954, 8.

183. "Start Work July 23 Grading Super-Road," *Greenville News*, July 23, 1936, www.newspapers.com/image/188667145/?terms=Grading&match=1.

184. "Employ 100 Men 8 or 9 Months," *Greenville News*, June 7, 1936, www.newspapers.com/image/188666911/?terms=grannis%20100%20men&match=1; "100 Men to Be Employed on Super-Road Job," *Greenville News*, May 21, 1936, 3, www.newspapers.com/image/188666356/?terms=grannis%20100%20men&match=1.

185. $2,000,000 Highway Between Greenville, Spartanburg Planned," *Greenville News*, June 18, 1935, 2, www.newspapers.com/image/188482699/?terms=super%20highway%20named%20for%20Byrnes&match=1.

186. *Greenville News*, May 2, 1936, 1; *Greenville News*, May 21, 1936, 3.

187. "Local Road One of Best in the Country—Super-Highway Is Given Nation-Wide Publicity in Journal," *Greenville News*, February 7, 1946, www.newspapers.com/image/187973124/?clipping_id=18022461&fcfToken=eyJhbGciOiJIUzI1NiIsInR5cCI6IkpXVCJ9.eyJmcmVlLXZpZXctaWQiOjE4Nzk3MzEyNCwiaWF0IjoxNzA3ODMwwOTYzLCJleHAiOjE3MDc5MTczNjN9.wluNRHtfLyx9Z7P3gpO_VWv5mdFqIdLkxjKcxtSHzYY.

188. "Bruce Seeks Job for Greer Mayor, Securing of Super Highway Through Town Be Issue-First Candidate," *Greenville News*, November 17, 1938.

189. "Action Is Taken to Bring About Complete Paving of Super-Highway; Stop Order Must Be Rescinded by War Board First," *Greenville News*, May 8, 1943.

190. "Road Department Launches Two New Super Highways," *Times and Democrat* (Orangeburg, SC), October 13, 1937, 6, www.newspapers.com/article/the-times-and-democrat/144974901.

191. Steve Frady, interview with the author, December 17, 2021.

192. Dot Arms, interview with the author, November 18, 2023; Shirley Beacham, interview with the author, November 20, 2023.

193. Department of Transportation Photographic Collection 833302, South Carolina Department of Archives and History, Columbia, South Carolina.

194. Paul Green, interview with the author, December 5, 2023.

195. South Carolina Department of Archives and History.

196. "Shrubbery, Evergreens, Roses and Fruit Trees," *Greenville News*, January 6, 1924, 22, www.newspapers.com/image/188214711/?terms=greenville%20nursery&match=1; "Selling Out Shrubbery—Greenville Nursery," *Greenville News*, September 28, 1945, www.newspapers.com/image/187978910/?terms=greenville%20nursery&match=1.

197. Richard Weingroff, Federal Highway Administration, email message to author, November 22, 2021. Weingroff is the Federal Highway Administration's unofficial historian.

198. "Mrs. Neal Is Hostess for Club Meeting," *Greenville News*, July 12, 1953, www.newspapers.com/image/190075967/?terms=Mrs.%20Neal%20is%20Hostess%20for%20Hampton%20Heights%20Woman%27s%20Club&match=1.

199. "Highway 29 Not Listed as Wade Hampton Boulevard: Name Used Frequently but Not Official Superhighway Title," *Greenville News*, May 5, 1950,

18, www.newspapers.com/image/191636994/?terms=wade%20hampton%20boulevard&match=1.

200. "Part of State Developing Seminole Trail to Be Talked," *Greenville News*, December 9, 1937.

201. "Sears to Build $450,000 Store," *Greenville News*, Saturday, May 22, 1948, 5.

202. Richard Sawyer, interview.

203. "Granite Markers on 29 Erected from City to NC," *Greenville News*, August 24, 1954, 5, www.newspapers.com/image/191218161/?terms=Highway%2029%20granite%20markers&match=1.

204. Thomas Hughes, interview with the author, December 8, 2024.

205. "Peach State," "Sweet Spartanburg Peaches," Visit Spartanburg, www.visitspartanburg.com/sweet-spartanburg-peaches/#:~:text=Byrnes%20declared%20in%20a%201951,friendly%20climate%20in%20the%20Piedmont.

206. Lemuel Dillard, interview with the author, March 3, 2024.

207. "Would You Like…," *Greenville News*, July 19, 1945, 13, www.newspapers.com/image/187974350/?terms=house%20super%20highway%20access&match=1.

208. "Close in Farm on the Super Highway to Spartanburg," *Greenville News*, July 1, 1946.

209. "For Sale: 10 Room House on Super Highway," *Greenville News*, January 28 1950, 14, www.newspapers.com/image/191592702/?match=1&terms=house%20on%20super%20highway%20.

210. "National Register of Historic Places Registration Form (New Hope Farm)," United States Department of the Interior, National Park Service, March 29, 1999, 7–8, www.nationalregister.sc.gov/spartanburg/S10817742043/S10817742043.pdf.

211. Jay King, "Historic New Hope Property in Wellford to Be Transformed by $50-Million Mixed-Use Development," *Upstate Business Journal*, June 2, 2022, upstatebusinessjournal.com/square-feet/historic-new-hope-property-in-wellford-to-be-transformed-by-50-million-mixed-use-development.

212. Laurel Horton, "An Upcountry Legacy: Mary Black's Family Quilts," Southern Spaces, southernspaces.org/2006/upcountry-legacy-mary-blacks-family-quilts.

213. Donald Jones, Startex-Tucapau Foundation, interview with the author, April 19, 2024.

214. Hughes, interview.

215. Joye Waddell Leopard, interview with the author, April 19, 2024; Amy Clarke Burns, "QandAmy: Bob Jones Land Before Bob Jones," *Greenville News*,

November 3, 2015, www.greenvilleonline.com/story/news/2015/11/03/qamy-bob-jones-land-before-bob-jones/75051418.

216. Paul Green, interview with the author; Sonny Rhem, interview with the author, January 5, 2024.

217. Joe Elliott, "Thunder Road: Remembering the Making of a Cult Classic," *Mountain Xpress*, May 4, 2016, mountainx.com/movies/thunder-road-remembering-the-making-of-a-cult-classic-in-asheville.

218. J.W. Williamson, *Hillbillyland: What the Movies Did to the Mountains and What Did the Mountains Do to the Movies* (Chapel Hill: University of North Carolina Press, 1995), 131, 190.

219. Author observation of memorial marker, Wood Memorial Park.

220. Lewis, *Divided Highways*, 45–46.

221. "John Steinbeck vs. Charles Kuralt: Who Said It First?" Highway History (Federal Highway Administration), www.fhwa.dot.gov/infrastructure/first.cfm, quoting John Steinbeck, *Travels with Charley in Search of America* (New York: Penguin Books, 1997), 70.

Chapter 7

222. Teresa Killian, "Steeple Is Closing," Go Upstate, October 13, 2005, www.goupstate.com/story/news/2005/10/13/steeple-closing/29347016007.

223. "Save Up to 40% on All Furniture at Culler-Jackson Furniture Company," *Gaffney Ledger*, February 5, 1959, 13.

224. "Why Is Culler-Jackson Closing?" *Greenville News*, July 25, 1978, 3, www.newspapers.com/image/189054498/?terms=culler-jackson%20furniture%20closes&match=1.

225. Richard Lane, interview with the author, March 20, 2023; Tony Waters, interview with the author, June 8, 2024.

226. Paul Green, interview with the author, February 2024.

227. Ibid.; "Put a Tiger in Your Tank," Woorilla Caught, www.woorillacaught.com/put-a-tiger-in-your-tank.

228. "The Esso Tiger: Roaring Through History," Garage Art, February 29, 2020, www.garageart.com/esso-tiger-signs-history.

229. Mike McMillan, "Benson Auto Museum Is a Tribute to 1950's Chrome, Culture, and Cars," *Greenville Journal*, October 20, 2022, greenvillejournal.com/community/benson-auto-museum-is-a-tribute-to-1950s-chrome-culture-and-cars; "Starting with $200, Jim Benson Built a Family Auto Empire Over 50 Years," *Upstate Business Journal*, August 14, 2014, upstatebusinessjournal.com/

economic-development/starting-200-jim-benson-built-family-auto-empire-50-years; Amy Clarke Burns, "Jim Benson's Drive Takes Him to Top of Auto Business," *Greenville News*, August 8, 2014, www.greenvilleonline.com/story/news/local/greer/2014/08/08/jim-benson/13777447.

230. William James Belasco, *Americans on the Road: From Autocamp to Motel, 1910–1945* (Baltimore, MD: Johns Hopkins University Press, 1979), 164.

231. Duncan Hines, *Lodging for a Night* (Adventures in Good Eating, Inc., 1954).

232. Gena Philibert Ortega, "The Real Duncan Hines—The Man, Not the Cake Mix," October 7, 2013, Genealogy Bank, blog.genealogybank.com/the-real-duncan-hines-the-man-not-the-cake-mix.html.

233. Belasco, *Americans on the Road*, 165–66.

234. Green, interview.

235. Lillia Callum-Penso, "After Five Decades, El Matador Continues to Draw a Good Crowd with Food and Charm," *Greenville News*, December 12, 2019, www.greenvilleonline.com/story/life/2019/04/01/greenvilles-el-matador-scs-oldest-mexican-restaurant-might/3106986002.

236. Donna Chandler, personal correspondence, March 4, 2024.

237. Peggy Edwards Harmon, granddaughter of Mrs. Monk, interview with the author, May 23, 2024; "Cora Lee McCarter Monk," Find a Grave, www.findagrave.com/memorial/39598363/cora_lee_monk.

238. "Dawson Dill Obituary," Greenville Online, www.legacy.com/us/obituaries/greenvilleonline/name/dawson-dill-obituary?id=48980248.

239. Belcher and Hiatt, *Greer*, 139.

240. "William Wesley Burgiss (Burgess)," Greer Heritage Museum Collection, Greer Heritage Museum, www.greerheritage.com/omeka-s/s/museum/item/3116.

241. Burns, "Q&Amy: Bob Jones Land Before Bob Jones."

242. John Matzko, "'This Is It, Isn't It, Brother Stone?' The Move of Bob Jones University from Cleveland, Tennessee to Greenville, 1946–47," *South Carolina Historical Magazine* 108, no. 4 (October 2007): 248, 251.

243. John Matzko, email, August 9, 2024.

244. Matzko, "This Is It," 255–56.

245. Huff, *Greenville*, 397–99.

246. Carole Greene-Henderson, interview with the author, June 30, 2024.

247. *Greenville News*, March 2, 1948 1; *Greenville News*, November 13, 1949, 4.

248. *Asheville Citizen-Times*, March 2, 1948, 3; *The State*, March 6, 1949, 37.

249. *Greenville News*, November 13, 1949, 4.

250. Ennis Davis, "98 Years of Winn-Dixie," The Jaxson, www.thejaxsonmag.com/article/98-years-of-winn-dixie.

251. *Greenville News*, November 17, 1987, 9.
252. *Greenville News*, June 22, 2005, 11.
253. *Greenville News*, September 2, 1945, 13.
254. *Greenville News*, October 5, 1958, 66.
255. *Greenville News*, February 4, 1958, 18.
256. *Greenville News*, May 14, 1949.
257. *Greenville News*, August 6, 1949, 12.
258. *Greenville News*, May 14, 1949.
259. *Greenville News*, August 28, 1949, 18.
260. *Greenville News*, May 31, 1959.
261. *Greenville News*, May 25, 1952, 49.
262. *Greenville News*, August 28, 1949, 18.
263. "N.E. Belmont Obituary," *Greenville News*, December 25, 1967.
264. *Greenville News*, October 9, 1952, 31.
265. *Kansas City Star*, January 10, 1991, 28.
266. *Greenville News*, September 4, 1952, 23.
267. *Greenville News*, October 8, 1952, 20.
268. "Sinclair Oil RD 119: The Miracle in Your Gas Tank," Comic Book Plus, comicbookplus.com/?dlid=3356.
269. *Greenville News*, September 24, 1953, 18.
270. *Greenville News*, September 30, 1952, 13.

Chapter 8

271. *Greenville News*, January 22, 1939, 21.
272. *Greenville News*, October 28, 1962, 1.
273. *Greenville News*, November 7, 1962, 1, 3.
274. *Greenville News*, October 20, 2017, A3.
275. Writers' Program of the Works Progress Administration, *History of Spartanburg County*.
276. *Greenville News*, January 6, 1939, 7.
277. "Shoeless Joe Jackson," SABR, sabr.org/bioproj/person/shoeless-joe-jackson.
278. *The State*, April 25, 1958, 29.
279. *Greenville News*, June 30, 2005, 24.
280. "MLB Stats for Dick Dietz," Baseball Almanac, www.baseball-almanac.com/players/player.php?p=dietzdi01.
281. "Carl Blair (1932–2018)," Johnson Collection, thejohnsoncollection.org/carl-blair.
282. Ruth Blair Lair, email correspondence with the author, June 3, 2024.

283. "Carl Blair," Johnson Collection.

284. Donna Isbell Walker, "Greenville Artist and Former Bob Jones Professor Carl Blair Has Died," *Greenville News*, January 22, 2018, www.greenvilleonline.com/story/news/2018/01/22/greenville-artist-and-former-bob-jones-university-professor-carl-blair-has-died/1055060001.

285. "Carl Blair," Johnson Collection.

286. Lair, email.

287. Brendan Blowers, "Houses of Good Design," atHome, May 18, 2020, athomeupstate.com/home-of-good-design.

288. "Carl Raymond Blair," Find a Grave, www.findagrave.com/memorial/186844139/carl_raymond_blair.

289. Marjorie Barr O'Steen, "Of This and That," *Greenville News*, March 21, 1954, 17, www.newspapers.com/image/191212359/?match=1&terms=daffodale%20

290. Alice Heitte, "4 Varieties of Daffodils Developed at Taylors," *Greenville News* April 7, 1963, 29.

291. William Gould Jr. Obituary, www.dignitymemorial.com/obituaries/clemmons-nc/william-gould-7519517.

292. Heitte, "4 Varieties of Daffodils."

293. Frances Worthington, interview with the author, February 22, 2024.

294. Frances Worthington, "Gardener Grows Designer Daffodils," *Greenville News*, April 23, 1995, 65, www.newspapers.com/image/192406175/?match=1&terms=designer%20daffodils%20worthington.

295. Ibid.

296. *The Daffodil Journal* 39, vol. 3, American Daffodil Society (March 2003).

297. Ibid.

298. "Eva 'Eve' Tate Robertson," Find a Grave, www.findagrave.com/memorial/41768985/eva-robertson.

299. Randy "Country" Hawkins, interview with the author, March 12, 2024.

300. "Carl Story and His Rambling Mountaineers Golden Anniversary," *Bluegrass Unlimited*, February 1985.

301. "Carl Story," Blue Ridge National Heritage Area, www.blueridgeheritage.com/artist/carl-story.

302. Hawkins, interview.

303. "Carl Story," Blue Ridge National Heritage Area.

304. Hawkins, interview.

305. "Carl Story," Blue Ridge National Heritage Area.

306. Nancy Snell Griffith, "Flint Rhem," Society for American Baseball Research, sabr.org/bioproj/person/flint-rhem.

307. Ibid.

308. Lula Dillard Rhem, conversation with the author, 1995.

309. William Lemuel Dillard (Flint Rhem's nephew), interview with the author, January 10, 2024.

310. Rhem, conversation.

311. "Flint Rhem, an Early Star," Clemson Tigers Baseball, May 8, 2016, clemsontigers.com/flint-rhem-an-early-star; author attendance, South Carolina Athletic Hall of Fame Inductee Ceremony, Columbia, South Carolina, May 16, 2016.

312. Gene Sapakoff, "Kidnapping, Drinking, and Happy Ending for Flint Rhem," *Post and Courier*, February 25, 2016, www.postandcourier.com/staff/gene_sapakoff/kidnapping-drinking-and-happy-ending-for-flint-rhem/article_b88b3407-9eb3-5a3a-86f3-cba9bbc78834.html; Sonny Rhem, interview with the author.

313. William Lemuel Dillard, interview.

314. "South Carolina Audited Accounts Relating to Isaac Green SC3446," Southern Campaigns American Revolution Pension Statements and Rosters, revwarapps.org/sc3446.pdf; Clarence W. Griffin, *History of Old Tryon and Rutherford Counties North Carolina 1730–1936* (Asheville, NC: Miller Printing Company, 1937), 133–4.

315. James M. Richardson, *Greenville County, South Carolina: Narrative and Biographical* (Atlanta: A.H. Cawston—Publisher, 1930), 247.

316. Robert Mills, *Statistics of South Carolina* (Charleston, SC, 1826, 1972), 572.

317. Alexander S. Salley Jr., "Sources Whence the Counties of South Carolina Obtained Their Names," *S.C. Legislative Manuel, 1946*, edited by James E. Hunter and Inez Watson (Columbia, SC, 1946), 335.

318. Huff, *Greenville*, 49.

319. Neva Turner, "Another Theory on City's Name (Letter to the Editor)," *Greenville News*, July 8, 1962 (clipped), www.newspapers.com/article/the-greenville-news-elisha-green-plantat/9989600.

320. Greenville County, South Carolina, Deed Book C, 63.

321. "The Upper Country of South Carolina: Historical Reminiscences of Greenville District, South Carolina, Etc.," *De Bow's Review* (New Orleans, 1853), 692–93.

322. "Phoebe West Green (1770–1868)," Wikitree, www.wikitree.com/wiki/West-4598.

323. Joye Waddell Leopard, interview with the author, April 19, 2024; Frank Waddell, "Like Sand in the Hour Glass (a Waddell history)," privately published, n.d., 4.

324. Joel Waddel, interview with the author, January 15, 2023.

Chapter 9

325. *Greenville News*, December 29, 1938, 3.
326. *Greenville News*, November 7, 1938, 2.
327. Nancy C. Yates, "One Man's Effort to Beautify Spartanburg," *Sandlapper*, March 1970, 40–42.
328. "The Dirt Daubers: A Brief History," Spartanburg Men's Garden Club, www.dirtdaubers.org/History.html.
329. Karen Nutt, "Famous Names Out There on the Streets," Go Upstate, March 2, 1999, www.goupstate.com/story/news/1999/03/03/famous-names-out-there-on-the-streets/29608298007.
330. Yates, "One Man's Effort to Beautify Spartanburg," 40–42.
331. Lynn Duncan's interview with Harry Corrigan, son of Douglas "Wrong Way" Corrigan, March 28, 2024.
332. *Lincoln (NE) State Journal*, November 10, 1940, 7.
333. *Greenville News*, November 15, 1942, 23.

Chapter 10

334. "Wade Hampton Boulevard Corridor Improvement Project," Greenville, https://www.greenvillesc.gov/2136/Wade-Hampton-Boulevard-Corridor-Improvem.
335. Ibid.
336. Ibid.
337. Cindy Landrum, "With Northpointe Shopping Center as a Catalyst, There Is Fresh Opportunity to Redevelop What Was Once Greenville's Main Corridor: Wade Hampton Boulevard," *Greenville Journal*, December 15, 2017, greenvillejournal.com/news/wade-hampton-anewwith-northpointe-shopping-center-catalyst-fresh-opportunity-redevelop-greenvilles-main-corridor-wade-hampton-boulevard.
338. "$9.5 Million in Spartanburg Earmarks Target West Main Street Corridor, Saluda Grade Trail Project," *Pal*, www.palspartanburg.org/latest-news/95m-in-spartanburg-earmarks-target-west-main-street-corridor-saluda-grade-trail-project.
339. "The Architecture of Refreshment," Martin Guide to Vintage Coca Cola Memorabilia, 1886–1969, www.earlycoke.com/architecture-of-refreshment.
340. Elise Devlin, "Coca Cola Plan to Be Revitalized in Spartanburg," *WSPA News*, January 14, 2023, www.wspa.com/news/local-news/historic-building-in-spartanburg-to-be-revitalized.

341. "Statues on S.C. Lawn Blasted by Gunfire," *Charlotte Observer*, Wednesday, September 20, 1939, 5; see also "Bullets Damage Spartan Nudes," *Greenville News*, September 19, 1939, 2.

342. "A New Era of Professional Baseball," Spartanburg Professional Baseball Club, spartanburgprofessionalbaseball.com.

343. "Morgan Square Design Concept," City of Spartanburg, South Carolina, www.cityofspartanburg.org/358/Morgan-Square-Enhancement-Plan.

344. "Morgan Square," SC Picture Project, www.scpictureproject.org/spartanburg-county/morgan-square.html.

345. Gabe Cavallaro, "3 Options for High-Speed Rail Route That Could Connect Greenville to Atlanta, Charlotte," *Greenville News*, October 28, 2019, www.greenvilleonline.com/story/news/local/2019/10/23/multi-billion-dollar-rail-could-connect-greenville-atlanta-charlotte/4052926002.

INDEX

ABOUT THE AUTHORS

 William (Lynn) Duncan (*left*) grew up in Travelers Rest, South Carolina. He got his love of history from his parents and grandparents. A retired educator, he worked for the Greenville County School District for forty-one years. He has done history-related presentations at the local, state and national levels. He is a member of the Circus Historical Society and has taught courses related to circus history in the Osher Lifelong Learning Institute (OLLI) at Furman University. He is the editor of ten oral history books, including *South Carolina Remembers World War II* (1995). He and his wife live in Greenville, South Carolina. They have two daughters and four grandchildren.

Scott Withrow (*right*) grew up in western North Carolina and got his love of travel from his parents. A retired educator and park ranger, he remains active in hiking, gardening, photographing architecture and nature, writing, pen-and-ink drawing and traveling. He volunteers with the Greer Heritage Museum, and he remains active in a number of local and regional genealogical and history groups. He teaches courses in history in the Osher Lifelong Learning Institute at Furman University.

Visit us at
www.historypress.com